MW01059717

Executive Coaching And

The Process of Change:

A Practitioner's Guide

By Alan G. Weinstein, Ph.D.

Alan G. Weinstein, Ph.D.
Professor Emeritus
Canisius College
Department of Management
Whele School of Business
Buffalo, New York 14208
716-491-3191
agw@canisius.edu
www.canisius.edu

Dedication

This book is dedicated to my parents, Sara and William Weinstein, who lit a fire under me at an early age and nurtured it through my formative years.

Table of Contents

Acknowledgements

No major undertaking can get done without many helping hands. I would like to thank three specific groups for their contributions to this book. The first group is my Canisius College MBA students who read early drafts of Chapters 1, 2, and 5. Their feedback helped to make these chapters clearer and more readable. Their positive reception also gave me confidence to continue writing this book.

The second group is my graduate students and colleagues who played a major role in creating sections of this book. Rita Markle worked tirelessly to co-write the article on which Chapter 1 is based, first as a graduate student and later as an executive coach. Amy Pearl and Sharon Randaccio, both experts in assessments, made major contributions to the content and writing of Chapters 3 and 4. Chapter 7 is based on a published paper written jointly with my graduate student and now colleague, Jessica Schimert.

The third group is made up of executive coaches who read and offered commentary on the manuscript. In particular, I would like to thank Dr. Dennis Gallagher, Dr. Adrian Geering, Jeannette Hobson, and Dr. Lawrence King for reviewing the manuscript with the reader in mind.

There were several lulls and surges during the writing of the book. One of the best decisions I made was hiring my editor, Steve McCabe, who not only made the book more readable but also helped me remain focused on completing the manuscript.

And, of course, no book can be written without the support of those closest to us. Thank you, Tamara, for tolerating me while I spent so many hours on this book. Your support inspired me. Your patience gave me the time to do my very best to share my knowledge and experience of executive coaching.

I take complete responsibility for the writing contained in this book. My hope is that this book will be a catalyst in promoting better and more effective executive coaching. Nothing would make me happier than the development and adoption of professional standards that incorporate the principles discussed in this book.

Prologue

My journey as an executive coach was not very direct or simple. When I reflect on my professional development, I am struck by one amazing observation: *I never had a coach.* As a youth, I yearned for a role model—someone I could look up to, a person I could model myself after, someone who could guide me.

That person was my mother. As hard as she tried to guide me, there were missing pieces that only a male role model could have provided.

In my early years as a professional, I yearned for feedback. I remember approaching a colleague who had been a leader in academic research in my field. I asked him how I was doing. His reply surprised me. He said, "I am not your supervisor"—in other words, I am not prepared to coach you.

My earliest attempts at coaching others were to offer advice. While I always had a need to help others, my style was to present my ideas but not always to understand the problem well enough to ask appropriate questions. Nowhere was this truer than in my own family, particularly with my children.

I am aware of three ways to approach coaching. The first is to tell others what to do. If you have authority and you want your way, you can bully and force others to do as you want. We are all aware of athletic coaches who use this approach. This dictatorial style is efficient and tempting if you really want something done and you are insensitive to the pain of others who may not want to do as you direct. The second method is to manipulate others. If you believe you can outsmart them or outmaneuver them, you can use your cunning to get your way. Powers of persuasion can influence others to come around to your way of thinking. This may get results, but it does little to help others become more self-sufficient and develop their own abilities. The third approach is to coach by asking questions and trying to identify a problem that the other person can work on. Through guided inquiry, it is possible to help a person to understand his or her problem and commit the time and energy to work on solving it. This is effective coaching. The role of the coach who employs this method is to help define the problem and not to do the problem-solving. It clearly puts the recipients of the coaching in the problem-solving mode, and it energizes them to do something about improving themselves.

As a teacher, I began my career trying to emulate the great masters in my field. The most obvious method offered to me was lecturing or presenting the best material I could find in the most accurate way I could communicate it. I judged myself on the content and accuracy of the information I conveyed as well as my ability to explain complex ideas.

I can remember colleagues complaining how their students were not very good. These colleagues almost always blamed the administration for admitting poorly prepared students. The evidence was clear to them: if their students could not master the material they were presented, they were poor students. There was little discussion of how to reach these students or how to adopt fresh ways of teaching them. The perceived solution to the problem lay outside of these teachers and with the student and college administration.

Some might call this behavior arrogant. This is true because the perceivers are trying to interpret the problem using their model of reality rather than trying to embrace the problem and learn from it, expanding their own model of reality. This form of arrogance is different from simple ignorance, which at least acknowledges that we don't know the answers.

I have learned a great deal from people in my life. My oldest son David has taught me the importance of individual differences. David has always been an original thinker. He did things his own way. I initially interpreted this as stubbornness and often used my authority as a parent to rein him in. I was arrogant in that I did not deal with David on his terms, but on mine. I had a mental model that I expected him to conform to. It took awhile for me to fully understand what I was doing and to change my approach. When I accepted him on his terms, my relationship with David improved markedly. David is succeeding today, doing things his way.

My youngest son Michael taught me the importance of appreciation in a relationship. Ever since I can remember, Michael had a deep need for affection. It is easy to be paternalistic as a parent, and, although you feel love, you may not demonstrate that love from a child's perspective. When Michael's brother left to attend private school, Michael showed signs of missing him and being down. He did not verbalize the loss, but it was obvious to me. I learned to focus in on Michael's needs and spent more time on his activities. This and a pet dog seemed to boost his energy, and he once again became his usually buoyant self.

My partner Tamara has taught me many things, but mostly how to love. I needed a great deal of introspection and pain to learn what must seem so obvious to many. It was through tough love, self-reflection, and the answering of some difficult questions that I finally learned how to love and how not to love. Having to reconcile my own behavior and manipulating others to my way of thinking, with my sense of well-being and need for closeness, forced me to recognize how I was chasing away that which I was trying to attain and save. Dan Baker and Cameron Stauth, in their book *What Happy People Know*, describe this dilemma in the following passage:

In the ultimate analysis, human beings have only two essential, primal feelings: fear and love. Fear impels us to survive, and love enables us to thrive. This complementary pair of feelings has been the driving force of human history (p. 80).

My first true coaching experience began when I joined an organization called TEC (The Executive Committee), which has been recently renamed Vistage. Vistage is a membership organization of over 16,000 CEOs and presidents. Members meet monthly in local groups and in one-on-one meetings with a chair who acts as a group facilitator and executive coach. As a Vistage chair, I started on a journey of learning how to ask probing questions and not jump right into a problem-solving mode. It also exposed me to some great coaches. Still, I muddled through, never certain whether or not I was truly helping my clients. Giving advice made me feel good and useful, so I often reverted to my helping behavior rather than effective coaching.

I have been greatly influenced by the work of many others. One book, *Now Discover your Strengths*, by Marcus Buckingham and Donald O. Clifton, had a particularly strong influence on my thinking. This book encouraged my adoption of the model of building on strengths and not focusing on overcoming weaknesses. One of the ideas from this book was that we often do not realize our strengths because they are natural to us. Likewise, we often expect others to have these strengths—not realizing that our own ease in these matters often leads us to assume that others have the same talent. Realizing my own strengths helped me to concentrate on what I do best. But, more significantly, it also got me to acknowledge that I spent far too much time doing things that I was not really good at. I would take on challenges that forced me to face my weaknesses and then regret doing so. I judged myself by what I thought I was supposed to be able to do and not by how fully I was using my strengths.

My work is a reflection of that of many others. As the coaching model developed, I realized more and more that I had been on a journey of learning and applying this learning to all aspects of my life. It was in many ways a personal journey. Joseph Jaworski, in his book *Synchronicity*, describes his journey from that of a successful trial lawyer to a pioneer in leadership development. In his journey, he found that the script he had followed for most of his career shut out most of the world from influencing him. His reality was limited by his mental model and the scripts he followed. His great revelation was that the world was open to him if he opened his mind and heart to it. It made all the difference for him.

I aspire to that same place.

—AGW

Chapter 1: A New Look at Executive Coaching: Reframing the Model[1]

"The thing that is really hard, and really amazing, is giving up on being perfect and beginning the work of becoming yourself."
Anna Quindlen

Executive coaching is a complex process within a rapidly growing industry. With the rising popularity of executive coaching, a comprehensive executive coaching model is needed. Without a comprehensive model, the quality and effectiveness of coaching will vary, which will negatively impact the overall value of the coaching process.

The Hay Group, a global human resources management consulting firm founded in 1943, recently reported that 60 percent of businesses currently offer some level of coaching services to their executives. It is anticipated this figure will grow at an annual rate of 40 percent. In addition, it is projected that the pool of executive coaches will need to grow from 10,000 to 50,000 in the next five years to meet the growing demand for executive coaching. You may be asking yourself, "What is executive coaching?" or "Why is executive coaching growing so rapidly?" and "What is its impact

---

[1] This chapter is adapted from Weinstein, Alan G., and Rita D. Markle, 2006, *A New Look at Executive Coaching: Reframing the Model*, an unpublished manuscript.

on the organization's bottom line?" Each of these questions will be addressed within this chapter.

The term "executive coaching" loosely encompasses all levels of coaching from mid-level to senior-level leaders. In this book, I will focus primarily on senior-level executives, such as the chief executive officer (CEO), chief operating officer (COO), president, and senior-level vice presidents, who by virtue of their position within the organization have unique needs and responsibilities. While this discussion can be applied to all levels of management, the examples offered will focus on senior-level executives. For the purpose of this discussion, I will use the terms "executive," "leader," and "manager" interchangeably.

What is Executive Coaching?

Executive coaching is an intervention process that enables leaders to improve performance and grow conceptually and behaviorally. When entering a coaching process, an executive must understand it takes time to create long-term, sustainable change. Coaching must capture leaders' aspirations and create pathways for them to reach their potential. Coaching is not about training, consulting, or mentoring; instead, it is best described as a dynamic and flexible iterative process for change that moves leaders from their current state to a desired state. Because coaching is a dynamic process, the issues and conditions being addressed at any given time may need to be reframed to focus on the future. This, in turn, may alter the original goals of coaching.

As an example, let's talk about a hypothetical CEO who is dealing with a marketplace downtrend that is impacting the longevity of the company's core product. The CEO knows it is crucial during this changing time to concentrate on both maintaining the company's current customer base and developing a strategy for the future. The coaching process enables this CEO to think strategically and focus energy on the competencies that are needed to make the organization successful. Once this strategy is identified, the CEO is able to re-focus on researching the potential of other markets, which leads to a shift in the organization's strategy.

In this instance, the CEO has reframed the current situation by projecting into the future and leveraging the organization's core competencies to develop new products and services with greater potential for growth. This intervention has kept the CEO focused on the marketplace, the organization's core competencies, and strategies for the future instead of only on damage control.

Why Is Executive Coaching Growing So Rapidly?

What is happening in organizations today to drive this current growth in executive coaching? Several factors are at play.

First, the role of CEO has become more difficult and complex, thereby requiring specialized skills. In addition, a growing segment of younger executives are starting new companies or taking leadership roles in established companies. These new executives may be entering senior-level roles with or without previous executive leadership experience or institutional political savvy. Executives today appear to be more open and less self-centered than their predecessors. They are more aware of the impact their emotions—and the effective management of them—has on their ability to be an effective leader. They are also cognizant of the importance of empathizing with others within the organization and relating to their needs. This has made them more receptive to learning and skill-development opportunities. They are ideal candidates for the benefits of executive coaching.

Secondly, some horrific failures in large companies today have raised a red flag to the business world and corporate boards. Company executives are becoming wiser, and time periods for newly hired or promoted executives to demonstrate competence and capabilities are getting shorter. Because of these factors, businesses are becoming more open and the performance of their executives more visible, which makes it more difficult for performance issues or fatal management flaws to remain hidden. Executives today are subject to both increased scrutiny *and* a finite timeframe for them to demonstrate their capabilities.

Thirdly, executive coaching is growing rapidly because the challenges facing today's businesses are emerging so quickly. Some of the challenges for CEOs and companies in this changing environment are technology, new markets, and fierce competition, which include the rise of global industries. The life-cycle of products and services has been reduced to a length never seen before. The time to market is shorter, and new products are becoming commodities much more quickly. The result of all these factors is that *organizations simply cannot afford to become complacent about their product offerings*. The current market is more turbulent, which means CEOs must stay focused and strategic rather than reactive and tactical if they are to lead their companies successfully today.

It's worth noting that, historically, coaching was viewed as a process to "fix" someone who was "broken." In recent years, executive coaching has shifted from being viewed as remedial or punitive in addressing performance issues toward being viewed more as mentoring or enhancing the capabilities of executives for achieving their most important business objectives in an increasingly complex and sophisticated business and leadership environment. Gone is any stigma that may once have been attached to executive coaching. Instead, coaching has become a proactive process, oriented and focused on ensuring the maximum growth of an individual's potential; it is a process that concentrates on preparing a business leader for the future rather than reacting to mistakes he or she may have made in the past.

Executive coaching is not a "one-size-fits-all" solution. It must integrate an individualized approach to effectively transform a good leader into a great one and position him or her to work more effectively while optimizing his or her capabilities. Executive coaching is now sought out not for those who are struggling but for the top performers whose growth potential has a high value for the organization. Organizations recognize the capability to make good leaders better—and even their better leaders the very best they can be.

Finally, the impact of coaching is both individual and organizational. For the individual executive, coaching raises personal awareness and encourages learning and innovative behaviors while nurturing a sense of ownership for problem-solving, goal-setting, and the building of implementation skills. For the organization, it aligns strategic goals with action, accountability, and entrepreneurial thinking. The combination of concentrating on the individual executive's strengths while building organizational alignment to ensure those strengths are fully utilized represents a significant shift in how coaching is being applied today.

Executive coaching is growing because organizations are recognizing increasingly that their leaders must become catalysts for change. Being a catalyst is a dynamic shift in behavior. It also requires that the executive focus not just on the immediate leadership tasks before him or her but also look ahead at the changing environment and try to predict how it is evolving. Executives cannot be focused solely on the "here and now." Instead, they must put energy into the dynamic role of their position and their market and business cycles, as well as look ahead at the uncharted waters. To expect executives to cope with market turbulence and stay focused on current issues while also looking ahead at future risks and opportunities without guidance, support, or continued feedback is unrealistic.

The Bottom-Line Impact of Executive Coaching

Is it possible to put a tangible cost/benefit to executive coaching? Exactly what *is* its contribution to the bottom line?

In the broadest sense, executive coaching will help leaders align what drives success in their companies with their leadership role toward that success. In the example described earlier, a CEO recognized his core product line was in a downward cycle due to emerging industry trends. His coach helped him to concentrate on what originally drove his organization's success. This led to the reinvention of the organization. By renewing his focus on the organization's core competencies, the CEO was able to expand its services into new lines of business.

Typically, CEOs find it difficult to take time out of their busy days to think strategically or creatively. Executive coaching promotes time for this type of reflection, which can lead to personal and organizational growth. For example, another coaching experience concentrated on a CEO who ran a scientific-based company. His executives did not know how to say "no" to customer requests. Hence, additional requests for work were met but never billed to the customer. This lack of billing for work performed led to erosion of profits and in some cases losses on major projects. Through executive coaching, the real culprit was uncovered: the organization's culture. An external consultant was hired to evaluate and improve the billing process, which led directly to an increased bottom line. But the key to this success was a coaching process that identified the real problem: this company's corporate culture was out of alignment with the realities of its business. As a result of his coaching experience, the CEO was able to drive organizational change focused on tighter billing policies and thereby improve the bottom line.

Types of Executive Coaching

A variety of types of executive coaching can be applied, based on the unique needs of the leader and the organization. It is important to identify each type and its impact. In a published handbook of best practices in coaching, *Profiles in Coaching,* the editors identified five categories of executive coaching ranging from behavioral coaching, to career/life coaching, to leadership coaching, to organizational change, and, finally, to strategy coaching (Morgan, Harkins, and Goldsmith 2003). The following is a brief description of each type of coaching.

Behavioral coaching focuses on helping leaders achieve positive, long-term changes in their interpersonal behavior. Most executive coaches specialize in this approach. Its purpose is to modify certain behaviors that may be interfering with successful performance.

Career/life coaching crosses the line between personal coaching and executive coaching. This coaching concentrates on personal growth, career development, and work/life issues. Time is spent on the intrapersonal life of the executive and may include study of personal values and development of a personal mission statement.

Coaching for leadership development helps leaders understand how their leadership style affects leader and team-member relations. It may also help leaders build a strong organizational team.

Coaching for organizational change engages the leader's capacity to effect change in the organization and the ability to develop alignment between the realities of the marketplace and the organization's response to it. It can also initiate changes in the internal structure of the organization.

Lastly, *strategy coaching* enables senior-level leaders to set the direction for long-term strategic growth in their organization. An executive coach must be prepared to work on strategic issues at this level of leadership.

Great executive coaches are able to engage leaders using all five types of coaching, depending on the specific situation and the leader's needs. This versatility is important to the effectiveness of the executive coaching process. As mentioned earlier, executive coaching is a dynamic process, and the direction of coaching may shift quickly from one leader issue to another. The coach should recognize this need to shift and respond accordingly. For example, an executive may shift focus from a strategic issue to an organizational-change issue. The coach will need to be equally competent to deal with both issues. There should be genuine concern when coaches with expertise and experience in one type of coaching take on challenges where they are inexperienced or poorly prepared. An effective executive coach must be competent in using all five types of coaching listed previously.

Measuring Success

Measuring the success of executive coaching is a difficult task. It is important to separate customer satisfaction from actual performance improvement when gathering measurement data. According to a 2003 Linkage Press Best Practices in Coaching Survey (Morgan, Harkins, and Goldsmith 2003), 78 percent of organizations currently measure the success of coaching based on accomplishing "the agreed-upon changes or objectives" and 69 percent on "satisfaction of the leader." To realistically assess the return on investment from executive coaching, the effectiveness of the coaching process itself must be measured, not other learning experiences that may have occurred during the same timeframe. In order to accurately measure the impact of coaching, time must elapse between the coaching event and the performance improvement to categorize it as a permanent change. To measure the permanent change, clear goals must have been created and documented from the beginning. Next, business metrics must have been established and tracked over an extended period of time. For example, if an executive were being coached on a leadership style that was causing increased employee turnover, then the long-term measure of success would be an increased employee retention rate and its potential cost savings.

Four Phases of Coaching

The coaching literature identifies many models of coaching available, and it has become apparent that there are many variations within these models. In order to organize these models and their variations, it is valuable to categorize them with four major "phases" of coaching: Contracting and Planning, Assessment, Intervention, and Evaluation. Each phase identifies a critical component of the coaching process.

Phase 1: Contracting and Planning

All executive coaching models have a contracting or planning phase. In this phase, the coach and the person being coached, or "coachee," identify the purpose of the coaching and come to an agreement on the goals and objectives. Typically, roles and responsibilities are outlined, as well as success measures. Following are the questions that must be addressed to develop an effective coaching relationship during the contracting and planning phase:

1. Who is the sponsor? (The sponsor is the person who initiates the coaching on behalf of the employee, such as a board member, CEO, or VP of human resources; alternatively, the sponsor can also be the coachee, if he or she is the CEO or other leader of the organization.)
2. What is the purpose and desired outcome for the coaching?
3. What are the measurable objectives, and how do they link with business and strategic goals?
4. Who else needs to be involved in the coaching process?
5. Who drives the coaching intervention?

6. How will the need for the intervention be communicated, and to whom?

7. Who will receive feedback, and how will the feedback be delivered?

8. What assessments will be used, and how will the results translate into a formal developmental action plan?

9. What is the leader's personal desire for change? (This last answer is absolutely crucial: *unless the leader recognizes and agrees to improve and change, coaching is likely to fail.*)

All of these components should be part of the initial contracting phase. The responses to these questions will clarify the coaching relationship and help create a blueprint for the overall coaching process.

Phase 2: Assessment

The assessment phase varies widely among the coaching models currently in use today. For example, Development Dimensions International (DDI), a well-known behavioral consulting company, advocates a full assessment, which acts as a baseline of the knowledge, skills, and abilities necessary for leaders to perform in their current roles. Relevant competencies for the executive's role can be identified using a 360-degree assessment designed to measure the perceived assets and liabilities of the coachee from multiple perspectives. Some of the coaching models suggest the use of multiple assessment tools, such as 360-degree feedback surveys, shadowing, behavioral-based interviews, simulations, personality inventories, action learning, and cognitive ability tests. Other coaching professionals merely observe and discuss the coachee's strengths and areas of development in the coaching process. During this phase, several models suggest that the coachee disclose his or her personal values and mission, plus interests, career aspirations, and outside influences. According to these models, it is believed that factors in someone's personal life have a significant and direct impact on organizational performance. At the very least, they certainly cannot be ignored.

Clearly, the assessment phase should measure the leader's current performance, strengths, and behavioral tendencies. The leader's desired state must also be clearly articulated to understand the performance gaps that exist. By measuring strengths rather than documenting weaknesses, a major shift in the coaching methodology occurs—one that focuses on leveraging strengths as the best way to achieving performance improvement. Studies by The Gallup Organization, authored by Buckingham and Coffman (1999) and Buckingham and Clifton (2001), and the writings of Seligman (2002, 2006) have created an awareness that people are more capable of improving when they concentrate on enhancing their talents and strengths rather than when they focus on eliminating weaknesses and deficits. Recently, Kahneman (2011), after reviewing the research, concluded it takes a great deal of effort to overcome liabilities, creating an energy deficit. On the other hand, he concluded that working on strengths may have the opposite effect of increasing energy. Of course, recognizing and making an effort at reducing one's deficiencies *is* important, but concentrating only on deficits reduces the success of the coaching results.

Phase 3: Intervention

Most coaching models incorporate an intervention phase. In this phase, an action plan is developed to create focus and accountability and to further define the coaching process. All the information that has been gathered in the previous phases is incorporated into the action plan.

Many of the traditional intervention approaches have been negative; they are often based on defining deficiencies that need remedy. As mentioned earlier, changing deficiencies is more difficult and limiting.

Often missing in the intervention phase of many coaching models is a strong emphasis on *how* to create change. It's critical to recognize that *change doesn't happen automatically*. The coach and the coachee need to establish the gaps between the coachee's existing behavior and the desired behavior. Once identified, these gaps then become the focal points for change. By identifying strengths and areas of development, the coachee will be in a position to create a proactive action plan to effectively shrink these gaps and enable movement toward their complete closure—and the desired behavior.

The intervention action plan should detail outcome-based goals, measurable objectives with business and strategic links, and proposed activities with realistic timeframes. Throughout the intervention phase, the coach should ask the coachee these three questions to ensure progress:

1) Where are you going?
2) Where are you currently in relation to your goal?
3) Are you currently on course to meet the desired goal?

These questions will serve to guide the coaching journey and keep it on track. This process will also reveal any obstacles or barriers that may impede success. Continuous dialogue, which includes asking probing questions and employing effective listening skills, is necessary to develop, implement, and maintain a realistic plan. Through the intervention phase, the coach is challenging the coachee in a supportive yet compelling way.

Phase 4: Evaluation
At the culmination of coaching, most models have an evaluation or review process to ensure that change has occurred. This component varies widely based on the specific model employed.

For example, some models assess change continuously throughout the coaching process to ensure that long-term, permanent behavioral transformation is occurring. Others only assess whether or not the specific goals of the coaching engagement have been met but do not track permanent change. But with either model, documentation, or some formal record of the outcomes of coaching, is recommended to provide evidence of progress in coaching and to reinforce its success.

Coaching is an iterative process. Long-term modification of behavior requires time in order for changed behavior to produce lasting results. As time evolves, behaviors can regress, which will require continual monitoring and further coaching. New challenges will often occur that can provide fresh opportunities for learning experiences, thereby helping the coach and coachee to reinforce desired outcomes.

In summary, coaching can be thought of as a dynamic process that moves through four phases. To meet the growing demands of coaching, an executive coaching model must include an initial phase that thoroughly outlines the purpose for coaching and its desired strategic outcomes. It must also identify the individual's behavioral or performance gaps that are creating the tension driving the desire for change. Coaching should concentrate on leveraging strengths while managing any liabilities. To increase personal expertise, coaches will need access to multiple diagnostic assessment tools. These will help to enrich the assessment phase. The intervention phase must establish a methodology for ongoing communication. An action plan should define the coaching process for the coachee and give the coach a map to chart progress and indicate junctures where intervention would be necessary. Finally, there must be a vehicle that measures and documents the change to determine the extent to which the coaching had long-term impact on the coachee's performance and the organization's effectiveness.

A vital component of the entire coaching process is a strong model for change. The coach and coachee must be focused on identifying the gaps that are producing tension and work toward transformational change to eliminate them. The strength of the coaching relationship will determine the success of the overall engagement. Therefore, there must be solid coach/coachee chemistry. Coaches must continuously encourage their coachees to leverage their strengths and recognize that their weaknesses may not be fatal flaws. Together, they must explore ways to overcome or manage the coachee's weaknesses.

Conclusions

When hiring a coach, organizations need to be concerned with validating the coach's expertise, ensuring a return on investment, determining the coaching needs, assessing the fit with the prospective coachee, and determining the appropriate timeframe for the intervention. Therefore, selecting and hiring the right executive coach will be a critical success factor for achieving positive, demonstrable results.

Chapter 2: The Coach/Coachee Relationship

"The wise man bridges the gap by laying out the path by means of which he can get from where he is to where he wants to go."

John Pierpont Morgan

In this chapter, a model of effective executive coaching will be presented by exploring three specific factors that influence the coaching process: the coach, the coachee, and the situational factors in the coachee's environment. In order for effective coaching to take place, all three factors must be in alignment. If the coachee interacts with the coach in a meaningful and productive dialogue about his or her situational factors, the intervention may lead to real change.

Coaching Assumptions

Coaching is a dynamic process between coach and coachee. For this process to be successful, the coach and coachee should have commonality of purpose and compatibility in behavioral style. This does not mean they must have the same behavioral patterns; it simply means their personal styles should fit well together so there is mutual understanding and the capability for open communication. Behavioral style becomes an important dimension of the coaching relationship that can either help or hinder the process.

The purpose of coaching is to bring about change. This requires an understanding of a change process that is embedded within the coaching model. Many coaches ignore the change process to the detriment of an effective coaching outcome. Coaching is not just *talking* about change: *it must also create change.* Everyone knows how difficult it is to create lasting change, but change, ultimately, is the true measurement of successful coaching. A coach needs to understand the processes that enhance the probability of successful change.

Effective coaching is also about excellence: how to recognize it, how to establish it as a common goal with the coachee, and how to chart progress toward attaining it. Striving toward excellence requires a great deal of "stretching" and ultimately contributes to potential pain and frustration as old habits are broken and new ones adopted. This can be a slow, agonizing process, but it is a necessary one for any successful outcome. Setting the highest possible expectations for top executives is essential to organizational success.

Effective coaching is also a learning process. The coachee is acquiring new behaviors and possibly new beliefs. Much of this learning is aimed at building confidence in the effectiveness of the new behavior. A growing number of professional coaches believe learning new behaviors is greatly enhanced by leveraging existing strengths rather than attempting to build strengths from weaknesses. This is supported by research cited in Chapter 1. From this perspective, coaching takes a different approach toward effecting change than traditional approaches. While not ignoring weaknesses, it is apparent that concentrating on strengths and ways to build upon them offers a higher potential for growth. Weaknesses are difficult to improve. To implement an approach that builds upon the coachee's existing strengths, the coach must focus on assessing those strengths—as well as any weaknesses of the coachee—and identifying the strengths that can lead to lasting change. In turn, the coachee's learning efforts must also concentrate on recognizing and building upon strengths while learning to manage weaknesses.

As the model unfolds, several additional assumptions will become apparent. These assumptions reflect the values that help to build the model, depicted in Figure 2-1. They are based on sound coaching practices and universal values of competence and personal effectiveness.

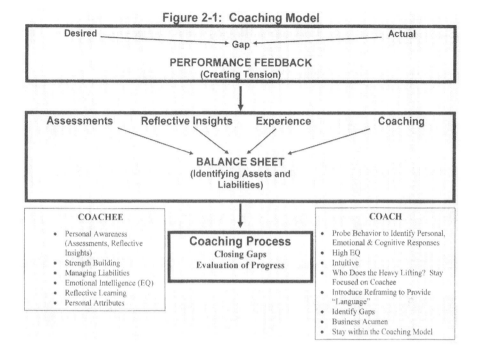

Figure 2-1: Coaching Model

Coaching Model

There are two ways to understand the coaching model being presented here. The first is to view it from a *developmental level*. How does the coaching process unfold as the coach begins preparing the coachee for change? The second is to view it as a set of variables based on research and practical experience of seasoned coaches. In other words, the coaching model incorporates attributes of the coachee, the coach, and the situation that engages both. I will refer to this as the *structural level* of the model.

Developmental Level

All coaching begins with a question or challenge. Generally, it begins with the identification of a gap between a desired outcome or behavior and the actual behavior. This gap should be the focal point of change, and the tension existing between the desired and actual states is the major focus of coaching. A key to success is to hold onto the desired outcome as the goal to be achieved. In some cases, this might increase the tension for the coachee. If the actual behavior is no longer tolerable at the level that the coachee aspires to reach, a powerful dynamic for change is created. The need to reduce the tension between desired and actual behaviors becomes the focus of the coaching relationship. What drives this dynamic is the motivation of the coachee to change and the ability of the coach to keep the coachee focused on change. This is not a new concept. It is a variation of Leon Festinger's Cognitive Dissonance Theory (1957) and Robert Fritz's Structural Tension concept (1984). Reducing this tension between desired and actual behavior becomes the work of the coach and coachee.

Once the appropriate gaps are identified, the coach then must assess the coachee's strengths, weaknesses, skills, and behavioral style and consider other variables related to how the coachee interacts with the environment. Chapters 3 and 4 are devoted specifically to the role of assessments and measures of assessment. Suffice it to say there are many potential assessment tools available to gain an understanding of how the coachee behaves under a variety of situations. These assessments are designed to identify potential difficulties as well as enhancers of effective behaviors. The assessments may also offer insights as to whether the coach is compatible with the coachee in a number of dimensions important to the coaching relationship.

Assessment tools are one way of assessing behavioral tendencies. Other methods of understanding behavior include readings relevant to personal insights, studying personal diaries, personal histories, and logs of insights gained through coaching conversations. These resources, and the insights gained from them, are a wonderful source of understanding behavior and its consequences. Combined, these methods yield insights that make it possible to develop a "balance sheet" of the coachee's assets, liabilities, and behavioral tendencies that will emerge as a resource for coaching.

Coaching requires specific coaching skills that must be considered when entering into a coaching relationship. These include the ability to probe the coachee with guided questions to help identify critical behaviors and patterns of behavior. Another tool is the use of reflective learning, which requires the coachee to reframe old situations with new models to understand how certain behaviors lead to different consequences. A caution is warranted here to prevent coaches from doing the "heavy lifting," which Susan Scott warns about in her book, *Fierce Conversations* (Scott 2002). Coaches may be excellent problem-solvers, but their role in coaching is not to be the problem-solver but the creator of insight and understanding so that the coachee does the problem-solving. This point emphasizes the fundamental—and critically important—difference between consulting and coaching, a point that sometimes gets confused in coaching situations. A consultant is usually hired to solve a problem or provide expertise in a content area. A coach, on the other hand, engages in a process that helps others to identify and structure their problem for solution. The coach's special expertise is in the methodologies of helping others to solve their problems. Good coaches work hard not to confuse this distinction between consulting and coaching.

There are many more attributes a coach should have that will be discussed in detail in later chapters. One that stands out initially is the need for the coach to be intuitive. Coaching is not a process of simply collecting all the data and then announcing the conclusion. Instead, the coaching process often works on hypotheses, hunches, or the ability to recognize a seemingly innocent comment followed by a line of questioning that may provide insight into a behavioral pattern. Coaches must use their intuitive skills to dig deeper into the triggers that may lead to change.

The coaching journey continues with development of an action plan that spells out all the dimensions of the coaching relationship. The plan should include specific goals for coaching, personal insights about the coachee and the consequences of his or her performance gap, measures for goal attainment that encourage accountability, some form of evaluation of coaching effectiveness, the application of new behaviors to situations, and feedback on the effectiveness of the plan as it is put into action.

Structural Level

This model defines the relationship between the coach, the coachee, and the situational circumstances of the coaching relationship. Many attributes could be included in this chapter, but the most important ones are listed below. Yes, there are probably dozens of attributes of an effective coaching relationship that are not mentioned here, but this model is a work in progress and is meant to be a starting point, not the last word.

Coach

No consensus exists as to what makes an effective executive coach. There are some attributes, however, that are important and, while not exhaustive, will be described in the context of the coaching relationship. First, the capability for self-assessment is crucial because it allows the coach to inventory his or her own strengths that are essential to coaching excellence. One such strength is the ability to work with a variety of behavioral patterns. The ability to recognize individual differences and incorporate these differences into the coaching relationship is another, and it is extremely important. The flexibility to vary one's coaching style to accommodate varied coachee behavior is likewise essential.

Several attributes can work favorably to support coaching. One attribute is intuitiveness. The coach must be able to sample verbal and nonverbal behaviors along with experiences of the coachee to understand how the coachee thinks (cognitive pattern), feels (emotional pattern), and interprets challenges and opportunities presented. Often the data are limited in these areas, and the coach must interpret only a few cues, drawing on experience and a feeling for the situation presented. Good coaches often find themselves putting forth a hunch of how their coachee thinks or feels in order to obtain clarification of the coachee's thinking and feeling. Unless the coach is able to generalize accurately from limited cues, the coaching can stall and break down.

For example, Tom is a top executive who struggled with giving feedback to one of his managers. This manager was not likely to be promoted to a job he wanted. The question addressed in coaching was "What is the basis of Tom's resistance to giving feedback to this manager?" It became obvious after several questions and some understanding of Tom's "balance sheet" of assets and liabilities, that the resistance was related to the lack of clarity Tom had in how to frame his feedback to the manager. This quickly led to the creation of the framework and practice in role-playing of the interaction and potential responses that the manager might exhibit. It also incorporated Tom's need to support the talents of this valued manager. To accomplish this, Tom was able to offer alternative growth opportunities that were a better match to this manager's strengths. When the conversation took place, it went surprisingly well, and the manager took the feedback with appreciation for its clarity and honesty.

This example demonstrates that there is no simple formula to suggest which track to take. Selecting an appropriate track is often an intuitive process that involves some guesswork and self-correction when it is off the mark. In Tom's case, overcoming his lack of clarity was only one potential approach to resolution. The ability to give good feedback is very complex. Identifying one approach that works is important but not necessarily the only way to success. Tom could have been confronted about his failure to give honest and candid feedback and how his fear of conflict and potential backlash from this manager kept him from dealing with the issue. But this approach would very probably not have brought about the desired result because it played to Tom's weakness and not his strength. Knowing Tom's lack of clarity in how to offer feedback to his employees helped the coach offer him a path to confronting his manager in a positive way. The lasting lesson learned from the coaching intervention is that Tom works best when he is able to frame feedback clearly with alternative outcomes.

Reframing is a way to create understanding by transforming or reinterpreting information into a more understandable framework. In the above example, Tom was able to reframe feedback to his manager into terms of meeting specific criteria for job success. Tom is an engineer who often deals with specifications for products. His manager is also an engineer. Tom was able to reframe the feedback into a specification and thereby have it conform to a familiar paradigm. The fit or lack of fit with established criteria for success was based on sound analysis and created a clear rationale for the decision. It removed much of the ambiguity and fuzziness that engineers like Tom struggle with and concentrated instead on specific criteria. This kind of ability to help coachees reframe situations is an important attribute of coaching. Effective coaches are skilled at helping coachees reframe problems, but they do not dictate solutions to problems. They use their probing skills to set up frameworks so the situation is understood from the coachee's point of view and is thereby solvable.

Another important coaching attribute is the ability to probe. Earlier, the distinction between coaching and consulting was established. A consultant is paid to solve a problem and is expected to give sound advice to the client. Subject matter expertise is very important to the consultant. Executive coaches should refrain from offering advice. Their role is to ask probing questions and to process the responses into a pattern so the coachee is able to understand and process the goal and determine his or her best path toward reaching it. In effective coaching, the coachee is confronted with solving the problem. Through asking probing questions and following the coachee's train of thought, the coach will help the coachee to frame the problem in a way that first leads to tension followed by resolution of this tension.

Emotional intelligence has become an important measure of behavioral maturity and leadership effectiveness. The work of Goleman and others has documented the importance of self-control, empathy, and social skills as components of emotional intelligence (Goleman, Boyatzis, and McKee 2002). The concept of emotional intelligence includes a set of skills that describe a person's ability to manage himself or herself and to engage others in meaningful and effective ways. Identifying a coachee's emotional intelligence and helping the coachee to use it effectively will enhance the potential for a successful coaching intervention.

A related body of knowledge important to coaching is learning styles. Different learning styles not only identify how people process information and learn but also suggest ways that coaches can relate more effectively with their coachees. Understanding learning styles will help coaches to develop empathy and better communication with their coachees. Learning styles will be discussed in more detail in Chapter 6.

It is difficult to conceive of an effective executive coach who lacks a substantial understanding of business. This understanding does not need to be industry-specific, although that may help in some cases. More importantly, coaches should understand the various roles of executives and how they fit into a larger business model. These roles are complex, and often very few guidelines define them. For example, the role of a CEO is not clearly defined. The early work of Carlson (1951) and Mintzberg (1973) helped to describe aspects of these roles. Several attempts have been made to define the role of the CEO, yet most CEOs will tell you they never found an adequate description to guide them in their role. In a conceptual model of the CEO role, Weinstein and Bianchi (2000) identified six areas requiring excellence in any CEO: strategic thinking, leadership, communication, managing change, understanding finances, and operational excellence. Each area included specific skills. As an example, leadership included motivating others and team development as well as coaching skills. Understanding the complexity of the role of the CEO is very important in helping the CEO to fully realize his or her potential. For any CEO, sometimes the dialogue is over finances; other times it may be over strategic issues. The ability to understand financial analysis and strategy is essential to executives who are responsible for these areas of their business.

A coach must have the confidence and trust of the coachee. This trust is based on the coach's ability to convey his or her commitment to complete confidentiality with the coachee. If the coach is contracted by a superior or board of directors, the question of loyalty and confidentiality of the coaching communication is always implicit, so it is critical to establish the strength of confidentiality very early in the coaching relationship. In a specific instance involving a company I had worked with, an executive coach reported confidential information from his coaching relationships with top-level executives. The coach's intent was to create candor. Instead, the effect was anger and indignation from the coachee at the breach of confidentiality. The coach tried to mend the situation but could not. Once confidentiality is breached, the trust necessary for effective coaching disappears and cannot be regained.

The change process as an integral part of coaching was discussed earlier in this chapter. Understanding change and how to bring it about is a crucial skill for a coach. The ability to identify tension or performance gaps that will lead to resolution and change is essential for a coach to be effective. This is why advice alone often does not work. Unless there is a compelling reason to change, advice is often short-lived or not heeded. Good coaches are able to create tension between desired and existing outcomes with enough emotional commitment to effect change. Overcoming resistance to change and helping to implement systemic change are critical to the change process.

Coachee

The need to understand the person being coached is fairly obvious, but how to structure a model with the attributes that require the coach's understanding is often far less obvious. It is helpful to break these attributes into three assessment areas: behavioral style, cognitive ability, and the balance sheet of strengths and weaknesses.

There are several measures of behavioral style. Some of the more popular assessment tools are DiSC (Inscape Publishing), Myers Briggs (Personality Desk LLC), and Workplace Big Five (Center for Applied Cognitive Studies). Most of these assessment tools measure several dimensions or styles. All three try to understand how the coachee approaches problems and situations. For example, DiSC, which is based on the work of William Moulton Marston, a psychologist who was with Harvard University, provides an assessment not of personality but rather of behavioral styles. DiSC measures the degree to which the coachee is decisive, goal-oriented, and direct (D score).

If an executive has a low D score, it suggests that his or her decisions may be slow and action stalled. It is not only helpful to understand the coachee's style but also the styles of other executives with whom the coachee works. If a coachee is a high D and works with a high C (someone who is cautious, risk averse, and needs to be sure before acting), friction can result over the speed and probable success of decisions. The high D is likely to make a decision before all the data are in to get to the goal faster. The high C is likely to hold back until sufficient data are collected to avoid errors and bad decisions. Both have a very different tolerance for risk. Knowledge of behavioral styles and how they manifest themselves is very helpful in understanding the coaching relationship. Chapters 3 and 4 provide more detail on how behavioral assessments can help the coach better understand the coachee.

Most people think of IQ when they think of cognitive ability. Cognitive ability also includes other skills, such as critical thinking, information processing, and specific aptitudes. The ability to create mental maps, have a vision for the future, and understand complexities are important attributes of the coachee. Cognitive assessments can help to guide the coachee to work on strengths and identify weaknesses that must be managed. Recently, an owner/CEO who could not grasp the concept of vision entered into a coaching relationship. He was not able to process an ideal or desired state. He clearly understood goals but only if they were specific and measurable. Rather than impose a mental model on this CEO that could not be understood by him, his coach instead helped him to create corporate goals and communicate those goals to others in a clear fashion. This CEO was also coached to understand that he may be placing limitations on his organization in both motivation and morale by creating a strong, operationally oriented company that lacked inspiration and a sense of greatness. He accepted this and now manages a very profitable, slow-growth company.

There has been a strong movement within the discipline of psychology to focus more on the positive and less on dysfunctional behavior. This movement has extended into management theory, somewhat reframed as concentrating on strengths rather than weaknesses. From a coaching perspective, strengths offer the coachee the opportunity to grow and succeed whereas weaknesses suggest remedial work and often failure, frustration, and lack of confidence. It is often a major revelation to executives that they can be far more effective leading from strength than spending time trying to eliminate weaknesses. Corporations have long based feedback to executives on their weaknesses and negative attributes. After all, the common wisdom is that strengths are expected and weaknesses need to be eliminated. This norm has become so prevalent that most executives hate to conduct performance evaluations. They also dread receiving them. The avoidance of candid feedback creates a major obstacle to improved performance.

Another revelation to executives is that it is okay to have weaknesses. Most executives are encouraged to hide their weaknesses out of fear that the company will hold them back or withhold opportunity if their weaknesses are revealed. It seems unrealistic to expect change within the context of a working relationship without having a candid, balanced view of a person's strengths and weaknesses. I will refer to this as a coachee's "balance sheet." We all have strengths and weaknesses. If we are aware of these attributes, we can begin the journey toward change. The balance sheet is the starting point of honest dialogue toward that change. I prefer using business language when discussing a person's strengths and weaknesses. By using a business metaphor, coaches can avoid the negative thinking that accompanies the concept of weakness. It also seems easier for business people to accept the concept of a balance sheet with assets and liabilities in place of strengths and weaknesses. This allows coachees to view their effectiveness much like a financial balance sheet. Coachees I have worked with like the concept of striving to always improve the net value of their personal balance sheet.

A coachee who has a realistic view of his or her balance sheet of assets and liabilities has an excellent opportunity to leverage assets while managing liabilities. For example, a coach has been working with Kevin, a top-level executive who is an introvert and very soft spoken. Some see this as a liability when it comes to inspiring or motivating others. Kevin's lack of charisma could be a serious challenge to his ability to lead his team and the organization. His coaching involved a balanced assessment based on a 360-degree feedback study that Kevin requested. From this feedback, reflection on past experiences, and the Strength Finder, an assessment of strengths based on research done by Buckingham and Clifton (2001), Kevin was able to create his balance sheet. Once he realized his assets—strategic focus, a thorough understanding of the operation, and trust and integrity—he was able to create a plan to leverage them. This was accomplished by sharing his vision and how he was going to help the company reach new heights with his team. He also shared his liabilities (even invoking the less judgmental concept of "less strong") and identified those on his team who could complement his assets and compensate for his liabilities. He was able to find more extroverted associates who became his disciples in communicating his vision and strategic plan for the company. Kevin still addresses the workforce, but he is clearly not as enthusiastic or animated as his appointed associates. Kevin is respected for his talents and his willingness to be a team player. His team recognizes his assets and admires his honesty and willingness to share in the leadership of the company.

Acknowledging assets and liabilities is important for a coachee. While such acknowledgment is a recognition of human vulnerability, it has the power to lead to a much stronger executive who must learn to leverage assets while managing liabilities in creative ways.

Situational Factors

Beyond the coach and coachee, there are several factors that influence the coaching relationship. One set of situational attributes is organizational. This includes how the company is performing, its organizational structure, its reporting relationships, whether it is a private or a public company, the role of its board of directors, and whether it is a family-owned business with significant family involvement. Any of these factors will have an impact on coaching. Coaches need to be cognizant of and comfortable with these organizational issues when they are present and applicable.

Family businesses present unique challenges to any coaching program. When coaching family members who have been selected to move into leadership positions in a family business, the dynamics of the intergenerational relationships, potential sibling rivalry, and whether the business or family comes first in important decisions all play a role in coaching. For example, Bob has been undergoing coaching, off and on, for 16 years. Coaching has helped him to accept leaving the company to complete his college education, gaining experience outside of the business, and developing a plan to learn leadership skills to ultimately be a leader in the business. Knowing his assets and liabilities, he wisely opted to allow another family member to become president, and he took on the role of vice chair and head of institutional sales, a role where he had strengths. He accepts his role as keeper of company values, protector of product quality, and co-decision-maker for strategic direction and financial matters. This was not an easy road for Bob to follow, with many difficult turns and decisions to work through. Understanding family dynamics was a key factor of the successful succession plan for this executive and company.

Other situational factors include the goals of coaching, demographics, timeframes for change, organizational support systems, managing crises, the challenges and needs of the business, and how coaching is perceived by the organization. Again, this listing of attributes is intended to be just an introduction and not the final word on what is included in the model.

There are many reasons for initiating coaching. Vistage International is a company dedicated to coaching CEOs and top organizational decision-makers. Vistage has identified several reasons for membership in its group, led by a chair who also acts as a coach. The acronym "MAGIC" is used to identify these reasons: Making better decisions, Accountability, managing Growth, dealing with Isolation as top decision-maker, and managing Change. Identifying the goal for coaching and measuring progress toward it is an important part of the coaching contract. For a coach to be successful, the coachee must perceive value. The clearer the objective of coaching and the more objective the measures of effectiveness, the stronger the coaching contract. This contract may be ongoing or a timed engagement, depending on the purpose for coaching (episodic or long-term developmental) and budget considerations.

Personal differences may include gender, age, race, and any other differentiator that has an impact on successful leadership. Volumes have been written about the relationship between these personal attributes and organizational success. A coach needs to be aware of the issues that relate to these differences. Coaches are not equally talented in dealing with diverse groups. Some attention should be given to gender, race, and age when selecting coaches to work with coachees. For example, the ability to empathize and identify with issues faced by women, minorities, and younger or older executives is important.

Coaching interventions can be episodic or developmental. Episodic coaching involves a specific problem or challenge upon which a coach may work with a coachee for a relatively short period of time until the challenge is met. This can be as brief as several weeks to a year. Clarity of expected results and knowing when these results have been realized is an important part of this coaching contract. Developmental coaching is longer-term coaching that is ongoing and without any particular timeframe. Many executives recognize the need for ongoing coaching to help manage the complexity of their jobs. They know that situations change, new challenges are always materializing, and ongoing coaching is essential to their success. This relationship is open-ended as long as there is perceived value. Some executive coaches have been successfully coaching developmental clients for more than a decade.

Organizations sometimes initiate coaching for executives as a means of creating change, but they rarely create the systems to support change. Take the example of John, a non-family-member CEO who ran a family business for years. He was creative and spent a great deal of energy to change the culture of the company. Through coaching, he realized this meant changes in the team of executives who were in charge of the basic business functions, such as sales, human resources, and operations. His owner often disagreed with John and sometimes failed to act on strong recommendations that would have strengthened the team. John felt he could not make the changes he needed to reach the expected organizational goals for the company. Frustrated, he resigned. John was caught with an unrealistic expectation of growing the company without the support he felt he needed to realize that growth. In this case, the coaching did not realize its potential because the organization did not support the coachee's recommendations. It is ironic that several years later, John became CEO of his former company's leading competitor.

Conclusions

Coaching is a dynamic process. It changes over time. For example, Peter is the CEO of a high-profile, family-owned-and-operated company; in his early years, his major issue was finding legitimacy in a company created by his father. The perception that he may have "inherited" his position often clouded his ability to demonstrate his own achievements. He wanted recognition for his own contributions and often found his father's style destructive to his attempts to lead. Over time, this issue abated and new issues emerged about his team, growth of the business, restructuring the source of financing projects, coaching his executives, breaking down barriers of departments that acted like silos, competition between executives, and working with siblings in the business. He also learned how to manage his own liabilities by creating organizational support systems while leveraging his assets of networking and business development. Today, he is recognized as one of the most powerful businessmen in his community. Over the 20-year coaching relationship, many challenges were met, and both Peter and the company he leads have flourished.

Coaching promotes change. This is not always perceived favorably. When a coachee attempts to implement change, organizational members often resist. Part of coaching needs to address the process of implementing change. Nevertheless, attempts at change are often ridiculed as "flavor of the month" or "this, too, will pass." The challenge for the coachee introducing change is to re-create the process that helped the coachee to change but do so on a much larger scale, within his or her organization. In other words, the change process or revelation that led the executive to change must be felt by others who are expected to change. This can only be felt when it is effectively conveyed by a coachee who is successfully implementing it to meet his or her goal of improving the organization. Shortcutting this process often leads to frustration and aborted change attempts. Clearly, coaching must deal not only with changing the CEO but also creating a process to facilitate organization-wide change. The organization must be receptive to change if a coachee is to have any success at leading that organization toward its goals.

In this chapter, the dynamics of coaching, both developmental and structural, have been explored and demonstrated. The developmental model describes how the coach can help the coachee create deeper understanding of self and the change process. The structural model elaborates on the attributes of the coach, the coachee, and the situation that are important to a successful coaching relationship. The following two chapters identify assessment tools to help both the coach and coachee understand the coachee's behavioral style, cognitive abilities, and balance sheet of assets and liabilities.

Chapter 3: Using Assessment Tools to Enhance the Coaching Process[2]

"Success in the knowledge economy comes to those who know themselves, their strengths, their values, and how they best perform."

Peter Drucker

The use of assessment instruments in the workplace has grown into a $400 million industry. In fact, more than 60 percent of *Fortune* 500 companies use assessments as part of leadership development. Their organizational development practitioners are blending the science of assessments with the traditional art of hiring, promotional decisions, succession planning, leadership development, and coaching.

This chapter will explore how assessment tools can be used to enhance the coaching experience, specifically by reviewing the following:

- The benefits of integrating formal assessment tools into the coaching process;
- A model for building an assessment toolkit; and

---

[2] This chapter is adapted from Pearl, Amy; Sharon Randaccio; and Alan G. Weinstein, 2010, *Using Assessment Tools to Enhance the Coaching Process*, an unpublished manuscript.

- Tools for measuring performance versus potential.

The next chapter, Chapter 4, will discuss the use of 360-degree feedback as a coaching tool, in addition to the following:

- How to select an assessment provider;
- Typical licensing and certification requirements; and
- A process for applying assessment tools in coaching engagements.

This chapter will also provide case studies illustrating the specific application of one or more of the common assessment tools in use today.

Benefits of Using Assessments as Coaching Tools

Assessment findings illustrate the traits and characteristics that one demonstrates on a daily basis. The data derived from assessments can help explain how an individual is perceived by others, what makes him or her successful, and what is preventing goal achievement.

Most leaders underestimate the impact they have on their organizations. It is a well-known fact that one of the major reasons employees leave their employer is not due to factors such as compensation or benefits but rather their manager's style

(Branham 2005). As managers climb the corporate ladder, they endure ever more pressure on bottom-line results and shareholder return. Yet, the technical skills, industry knowledge, and attributes that got them to their current role are probably not going to take them to the next level. In fact, over 40 percent of new managers fail within 18 months (Right Management, Inc., 2011). Most of these failures are due to an inability to build good relationships, or develop "emotional intelligence," a term coined by Daniel Goleman. Many factors can cause managers to derail. And ironically, senior managers tend to get less behavioral feedback at a time when it is most needed—as they assume growing responsibilities in their movement up the corporate ladder.

When used appropriately, feedback creates the gift of self-awareness. Individuals can identify their personal assets and liabilities. They can see what is derailing them. Every day, wise leaders use information to understand their businesses and to make the changes to achieve their business goals. Similarly, wise leaders use personal assessment information to understand their styles and to guide meaningful behavioral change.

In summary, for coaching, the benefits of using assessments are many.

Self-Assessment for the Coach

To start, every coach must look in the mirror. The coach needs to understand his or her own style, be able to identify the style of the coachee, and be nimble and flexible enough to facilitate the coaching process. The coach must reflect on his or her own style to determine its compatibility with the coachee's and to be aware of any blind spots that may exist when coaching others. Building trust is one of the most important elements of a coaching relationship. Assessment data facilitates the ease of establishing rapport and being authentic—two key ingredients for a trusting relationship.

If you are a coach, creating your own personal balance sheet, comparable to one you will create with the coachee, is a priority. What assets do you bring to the table that can benefit your coachee? Are you a strong listener, supportive counselor, creative idea generator, tough challenger, change agent? How can these assets contribute to a positive coaching outcome?

On the contrary, what are your liabilities? How can your style keep your coaching engagements and practice from being as successful as possible? What can you do to develop or compensate for those shortcomings?

It is easy to build a strong relationship when the coach and coachee have a strong compatibility in behavioral style. Yet, this doesn't mean that the coach and coachee need to have the *same* style. In fact, the following case study illustrates how two different styles can create an effective dynamic between the coach and coachee.

Case Study: The Accommodating Manager Meets the Challenging Coach

Many times, an individual is promoted to a management position as a result of strong job skills. Such was the case with Mary, a registered nurse who was promoted to director of nursing for a large hospital. As a nurse, Mary's helpful, supportive nature led to many accolades from patients and physicians. However, the hospital was faced with financial challenges driven by low reimbursement rates and lack of efficiency. As the director of nursing, Mary was responsible for improving efficiency without compromising quality, as reimbursement rates were not projected to increase.

Mary's nursing teams were averse to change, and she found herself accepting their excuses for not being able to achieve the new goals. As a result, Mary was failing in her work and feeling like she had made the wrong choice in accepting the director position.

Recognizing her strong strategic-thinking abilities and industry knowledge, the hospital administrator extended the opportunity for Mary to work with a coach to overcome her leadership challenges.

Through Mary's assessments, the coach was able to illustrate that Mary was extremely accommodating and service-oriented, and she had a tendency to yield in conflict. Although these were assets in her role as a registered nurse, they became liabilities in her new role. The coach used the assessment data to stimulate dialogue. Mary confided in the coach that she was uncomfortable when the nurses pushed back and when having discussions with poor performers.

On the other hand, the coach was always known as a challenger, someone who questioned the status quo and acted as a change-agent. Throughout the coaching engagement, the coach encouraged Mary to identify changes that needed to be made, helped her to create a process for getting commitment from skeptical staff members, rehearsed difficult conversations, and provided a system of accountability for seeing changes through to completion.

However, there was great risk in this relationship. The coach's challenging style could have easily pushed Mary to be turned off by these more aggressive management techniques. And, the coach could have lost patience with Mary's conflict-averse nature.

To keep this from happening, the coach reflected on her own personal style before each coaching meeting. She challenged Mary to be more aggressive, but only in a sensitive, cautious manner. She carefully walked Mary through specific examples of the situations she faced, asked probing questions, and responded with empathy. She encouraged Mary to take small steps at first, to build confidence in her ability to make changes. Over time, Mary came to appreciate the coach's challenges and worked with her to create change. She found the right balance to achieve her goals by borrowing some techniques and style-pointers from her coach.

Assessment Benefits for the Coaching Process

The coach's own self-assessment builds the foundation for assessing the needs of the coachee and establishing an effective coaching relationship with him or her. The following are some of the most significant benefits of assessment tools to the coaching process.

Assessment Provides Shortcuts to Understanding the Coachee: As discussed in the previous chapter, the process of developing the coachee's balance sheet provides the coachee with tools to improve performance. Once the coaching challenges are established by identifying the tension created between desired levels of performance and actual levels of performance, assessments will provide clues to how the coachee approaches situations and his or her potential for change. This requires reflection on past experiences and personal attributes. Formal assessment tools provide a comprehensive, efficient, and objective mechanism for measuring a coachee's skills, behaviors, potential, preferences, and style, allowing a coach to probe deeper and to build the coachee's balance sheet. This will allow the coach to better understand current challenges and to use the balance sheet as an instrument for change. This process provides the coach with insights to ask probing questions that may verify assessment findings and to relate these findings to the coachee's desire for change.

Assessment Provides Valid Insights for the Coachee: Creating self-awareness is one of the initial steps of a coaching process. It can also be one of the most difficult steps. As the case study below illustrates, coachees may not be in touch with their true talents or how they are perceived by others. Coachees gain invaluable insights in these areas from assessment reports. A skilled coach presents even the most sensitive feedback in a user-friendly, objective, and actionable format.

Case Study: The Tough Perfectionist Changes His Approach

Kevin owned a real estate development company with a staff of 20 employees. He initially engaged a consultant to build a compensation system to help eliminate the many instances of poor accountability among his team. Kevin reported that no one at the company could be trusted to execute a task without error. As a result, he was micro-managing each person, leading to excessive stress at the office and in his personal life. Kevin was unable to grow the business because the team couldn't even handle the workload of the business at its current size. While in the waiting room, the consultant would often overhear very heated discussions between Kevin and his team members.

The consultant realized that the accountability problems were just symptoms of larger issues. She successfully persuaded Kevin to try a personality assessment. In debriefing him on the results, the consultant showed Kevin that:

- *He was in the top quartile of perfectionists, with expectations far beyond average.*
- *His reliance on conflict and authority was creating win-lose relationships with people.*
- *His stress level was dangerously high for his company, his team, his family, and himself.*

The consultant shifted roles and became Kevin's coach. On a daily basis, Kevin was able to see his assessment traits play out in his work, as well as the effects of these traits on others. However, these personality traits were so deeply ingrained in Kevin's core that they would be difficult to change. Realizing that Kevin was unwilling to compromise his high standards, the coach challenged him to select personnel who were more closely aligned with his expectations.

Kevin needed a team of competent professionals he could trust. Although this took time, he eventually hired individuals who met his expectations. The coach helped Kevin to utilize assessments while hiring by designing interview and reference-check questions to test for style and ensuring that Kevin gave job candidates a realistic preview of his expectations and his style.

In time, Kevin built a stronger team. Competent individuals who shared Kevin's high standards were hired. The new team members also had higher expectations for their own work environment. The coach worked with Kevin to design a more collaborative and less hierarchical organizational structure while helping Kevin develop techniques for creating win-win situations. Although still an individual who challenges others, Kevin learned to debate and to discuss rather than to dictate or argue.

The resulting changes enabled Kevin to expand his business internationally. More importantly, he is managing his stress effectively, leading to both professional and personal benefit. This success would not have been achieved if the coach had tried to change Kevin's personality. Instead, she helped him develop the tools and techniques to create an environment that maximized his strengths.

Assessment Stimulates Reflection and Analysis: The comprehensive nature of an effective assessment process causes coachees to examine their assets as well as their liabilities. They may see skills they have not used in years, hidden potential in attributes they have not fully developed, triggers that cause both positive and negative emotional responses, and other indicators of behaviors in both professional and personal settings. Effective coaches can use assessment reports to ask probing questions and enable the coachee to identify specific situations where he or she has seen his or her assets and liabilities in play.

Assessment Facilitates an Individualized Coaching Approach: No two individuals are alike. Similarly, coaching processes must be customized to fit the unique needs of the individual. The right combination of assessment tools will yield a profile that demonstrates the unique attributes of the coachee, giving the coach an opportunity to tailor interventions to target the specific needs of the individual.

Assessment Provides a Team View: Self-awareness is a crucial step, but coachees can also benefit from understanding their bosses, peers, direct reports —*even their spouses and life partners.* The use of assessments in the coaching process for other members of the team can hasten the learning process for the coachee and provide opportunities for group coaching, team building, or mediation.

Skilled coaches are prepared to work with groups and often facilitate sessions with their coachee and his or her team. Topics for group sessions can include identifying the competencies necessary for future success, identifying team assets and liabilities, valuing and capitalizing on the unique traits of individual team members, and building stronger communication despite opposing styles.

Assessment Produces Metrics for Success: You can't manage what you can't measure—and if you can't manage it, you leave success to chance. Assessments provide metrics—valid and reliable measures of an individual's most important attributes. Assessment scores help to benchmark strengths and identify areas for improvement. And, 360-degree feedback tools, which will be discussed later, in Chapter 4, can be utilized throughout the development cycle to gauge progress. Follow-up 360-degree feedback will demonstrate whether or not coaching has led to desired results.

In sum, assessments can greatly enhance the coaching process by providing insights and clues to help both the coach and coachee create the framework for change.

The Assessment Hierarchy

A simple internet search of the word "assessments" reveals over 42 million results. And, different assessments have different purposes and answer different questions. So, identifying the right assessment tools can be a daunting task. Figure 3-1 presents a model to help organize one's thoughts when building an assessment toolkit.

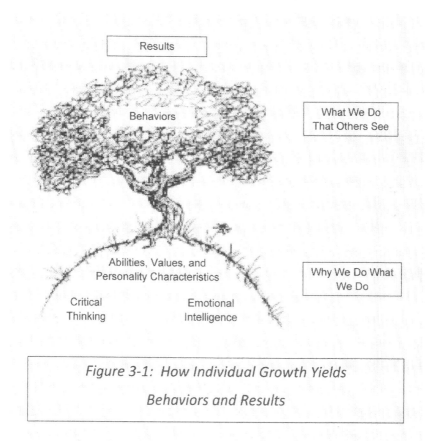

Figure 3-1: How Individual Growth Yields
Behaviors and Results

Ultimately, each coachee is trying to achieve improved results. Those results might be achieving specific business goals, building a stronger team, being promoted to a new position, or finding a better work/life balance. Although successes and failures can be influenced by external factors, often an individual's results rest upon his or her ability to demonstrate the right behaviors.   And, it's easy to see how an individual's behaviors can impact results:

- The persistent and competitive salesperson who is not dissuaded by prospects who turn him down and who effectively overcomes objections to close sales and achieve his sales goals.
- The project manager who uses a disciplined approach, careful planning and status tracking, and regular project team communication to successfully implement a new solution.
- The customer service representative who effectively balances execution of company policy with empathy to meet customer needs while managing company risk.

It's also easy to see the behaviors that cause negative effects:

- The quiet co-worker who fails to share good ideas with the rest of the team.
- The employee who doesn't pay attention to the details or complete the required paperwork to support his or her work.
- The manager who enthusiastically accepts new tasks but doesn't follow them through to completion.

One of the simplest and most cost-effective assessments for discovering behavioral preferences is the DiSC personal profile system. It provides insight into an individual's behavioral tendencies by measuring four dimensions of his or her behavior: results-oriented "Dominant," relationship-oriented "Influence," team-oriented "Steadiness," and quality-oriented "Conscientiousness." Coachees find they can build effective interpersonal relationships by learning to read people by understanding their behaviors and by adapting their own behaviors to meet the needs of others. Many DiSC-based assessment tools are on the market.

It's important to note that many behaviors are observable in the activities of individuals. Yet often, behaviors may be hidden, and it is difficult to explain an individual's actions. Figure 3-1 shows that individual behaviors are often driven by other factors, like critical thinking skills, core values, and personality. Since these behavioral drivers are beneath the surface, they are more difficult to see and explain. It is important to know that they can be much more difficult to change than our surface behaviors. Assessment processes and formal assessment tools help to measure, understand, and articulate behavioral drivers.

The following section of this chapter explains the drivers of behavior and provides examples of assessments that can be utilized to enhance the coach's toolkit.

Personality

Personality is at the base of observed behaviors. Continuing research is aimed at determining the degree of inheritability of personality factors. Neubauer and Neubauer (1990) have published considerable research on the genetic origins of personality traits. Some traits show strong evidence of inheritability. Traits such as imagination, aggressiveness, vulnerability to stress, empathy, and excitability are examples of traits that appear to have a hereditary basis. They will be very difficult to change. This was seen in the previous case study of Kevin, whose stress over the pursuit of perfection and excitability led to heated arguments in the office. Kevin was unable to change his heightened sensitivity for perfection. Instead, he identified triggers and created an environment where those triggers were minimized, thereby compensating for a major liability on his personal balance sheet. In the hands of a skilled coach, personality assessments can help provide a vehicle for change. The secret of success in such instances is to not attempt to change personality but instead to reframe a situation or find other means of circumventing the negative consequences of a personality characteristic.

Consider the following case of Jim for an example of how coaching helped reconcile personality with goals.

Case Study: The Physician's Dilemma

Pushing individuals to behave in ways that are not inherently driven by their personalities can lead to unsatisfying and unrewarding careers. Such is the case with Jim, a physician, whose rapidly expanding medical practice required him to increase the amount of time spent managing business issues. Since his time spent on business matters was taking him away from patient appointments, revenue was decreasing. This prompted him to engage a coach to help him improve his medical practice management techniques.

Through various assessments, Jim learned that:

- *He had a thirst for knowledge and learning associated with the academic research he used to enhance his patient outcomes. However, his time for this research was now severely limited.*
- *He didn't trust easily. His skeptical nature was an attribute that contributed greatly when diagnosing patients and recommending treatments. However, this same skepticism made it difficult for him to delegate important business matters to someone else.*
- *His emotional intelligence was below average, particularly in the areas of self-awareness and interpersonal relationships.*

Jim realized that his personality fit perfectly with his role as a physician and leveraged these traits as an asset. Yet, these traits were liabilities as a manager. Spending time on business management tasks was not just financially draining but personally draining as well. Jim worked with his coach to build a practice model that maximized his patient care and research time. He learned to manage his liabilities by carefully hiring a practice administrator, holding group coaching sessions (coach, physician, and practice administrator) to establish open communication, sharing expectations, and building systems of accountability such that a strong, trusting relationship was achieved. In addition, Jim's medical practice increased its revenues while his administrative burden eased.

Examples of Personality Assessment Tools

There are many personality assessment tools on the market. We have selected three of the more popular tools to illustrate how personality can be assessed.

The previously mentioned Myers Briggs Type Inventory (MBTI) is one of the most widely used personality inventories. The MBTI determines preferences on four dichotomies: extroversion/ introversion, sensing/intuition, thinking/feeling, and judging/ perceiving. Combinations of these preferences result in categorization of 16 distinct personality types. Understanding these characteristics provides insight into how they influence an individual's way of communicating, making decisions, and interacting with others.

More robust tools are based on the widely published Five-Factor Model of personality (FFM), or the Workplace Big Five Profile. What separates this assessment from all others is that it is not based on the theory of any one particular psychologist but rather on the language of the workplace, the natural system that people use to communicate their understanding of one another at work. A number of meta-analyses have confirmed the predictive value of the Workplace Big Five across a wide range of behaviors.

Hogan Assessment Systems also offers a variety of reports, including the assessment Hogan Personality Inventory (HPI) as well as the Hogan Development Survey (HDS), which explores potential career impediments. This tool explores likely behavior for individuals under pressure or in the face of danger. As stated by Robert Hogan, the company's CEO, "Every leader has personality characteristics that threaten his or her success."

Often, too much of an individual's given asset can actually become an impediment. For example, a manager who is extroverted may be an excellent communicator. When under pressure, the manager draws even more on extroversion, resulting in others viewing him as a poor listener. Similarly, a desirable characteristic in a manager is the ability to stay calm and cool under pressure.

However, this could become a problem if, in the face of a significant challenge, the manager is perceived as being so laid back that he or she shows little urgency and is unable to connect with staff.

Research indicates that failed managers are less self-aware, have inflated self-evaluations, easily lose composure, handle mistakes defensively, and are unable to learn from experience (Eichinger and Lombardo 2003). Assessing the "dark side" of a manager's personality may identify such potential impediments to his or her success. Knowing this can help a coach to find other ways of guiding a manager toward success.

Values

Values are a statement of what is important to an individual. Values form the core of our identity—our need to get along, our need to get ahead, and our need for meaning. Values influence our thinking, feelings, and, in part, our behavior. Values tell us what we enjoy doing and what motivates us, such as recognition, power, affiliation with others, financial success, variety, or excitement. Values determine the kinds of environments in which an individual will best perform, as well as the kind of culture the person will create as a leader. People perform better when their personal values are consistent with their company's values and culture.

Values can be measured. The Hogan Motives, Values, Preferences Inventory (MVPI) explores an individual's core values and goals to help define the environment in which a person is most likely to excel as well as the kind of culture an individual might create as a leader.

Critical Thinking Skills

Critical thinking skills help individuals process what they see and hear and turn that information into meaningful, actionable responses. Critical thinking skills differ from an Intelligence Quotient (IQ), which typically measures mathematical and spatial reasoning, logical ability, and language understanding. Critical thinking includes an ability to define complex problems and situations, identify information needed to enhance decision-making, apply sound logic when analyzing information, and draw accurate conclusions from information. Individuals with strong critical thinking skills have strong verbal reasoning ability and are able to "connect the dots" and see the big picture when dealing with strategic issues. Critical thinking can be measured and is another dimension that drives behavior.

One of the most widely used assessments of critical thinking is the Watson-Glaser Critical Thinking Appraisal. It is ideal for hiring, promotion, development and succession planning for management, and other roles requiring an individual to work with business information to answer questions, determine strategy, and reduce risk. This tool will help a coach to predict how well a coachee will make accurate inferences, recognize assumptions, properly interpret information, and evaluate alternative positions.

Emotional Intelligence

Emotional intelligence is the basis for our social interaction. It allows us to perceive, generate, and manage emotions in ourselves and others. Individuals with high emotional intelligence (often abbreviated as EI or EQ) communicate effectively, form strong relationships, manage their impulses, and have a positive outlook. Managers with low emotional intelligence typically have poor self-regulation and weak interpersonal skills.

A leading researcher and author, Daniel Goleman, has popularized emotional intelligence. He asserts that people are hired for their technical abilities but promoted for their emotional intelligence. He often tells of a manager at AT&T's Bell labs who was asked to rank his top performers. They weren't the most brilliant engineers but rather the individuals who were good collaborators and networkers and were popular with their colleagues.

Many self-help books and Internet sites contain simple assessments of emotional intelligence traits. One of the most widely used formal assessments of emotional intelligence is the Bar-On Emotional Quotient Inventory (EQ-i). Participants in the EQ-i self-report in 15 key areas of emotional skill—from independence to empathy to flexibility to stress tolerance. These skills determine proficiency in such complex business functions as conflict resolution and negotiation.

An alternative tool is the Mayer-Salovey-Caruso Emotional Intelligence Test (MSCEIT). Coachees analyze scenarios typical of everyday life and respond to questions with the direct application of emotional intelligence. The results, consequently, provide an immediate view of actual emotional intelligence capability and performance.

By studying the various attributes of emotional intelligence, coaches can guide their coachees to leverage the EQ characteristics in which they excel while managing those characteristics in which they are deficient or perhaps draw on another strength as a means of managing the liability.

For example, a father was having difficulty with a young son who was rebellious. The father struggled with demonstrating empathy, a key EQ attribute. He could not understand or appreciate his son's behavior. However, he was an extraordinarily focused individual. The father used this asset to concentrate on his son's needs rather than his behavior. He spent quality time with him and engaged in activities that the son enjoyed. By doing so, he was able to improve his relationship with his son, which greatly lessened the rebellious behavior.

Past Experiences, Knowledge, and Skills

Past experiences, knowledge, and skills also shape the ability to perform, as well as the way a person behaves in current situations. Such is the case when the routines, practices, and mannerisms learned in previous places of employment are carried to a new job. Sometimes, the methods in use at one company are very different from the methods of another. Similarly, the behaviors acceptable at one place of employment may not fit the culture at another.

Knowledge and skills are also contributors to an individual's ability to perform. Does the individual know how to achieve the goals and behave in the manner that is expected? Knowledge and skills are typically gained through training, education, self-learning, and other life opportunities.

Although tools are available to assess specific competencies, many coaches find that probing and reflection are enough to gain crucial insight as to how a coachee's experiences, knowledge, and skills are impacting his or her current situation. Reflection is a powerful method to identify how past experiences relate to current behaviors. Some coaches challenge coachees to reflect on their past to identify the earliest occurrences of a pattern of behavior. The individual is led through a process to identify how the drivers of these behaviors are no longer present and to eliminate the vestiges of the behaviors that are no longer necessary. Even though this chapter encourages the use of formal assessment tools, coaches should not sacrifice the opportunity to have meaningful discussions with their coachees to identify drivers of job behaviors. Chapter 5 offers a detailed process for coaching through reflection.

How Much Can Be Changed?

As the previous discussion illustrates, personality, values, critical thinking, emotional intelligence, and past behaviors are all drivers of current behavior. These attributes of the individual can be difficult, if not impossible, to change.

The motivation to change comes from within an individual. However, a coach can strive to create an environment that influences the coachee to change. Creating self-awareness through assessments is an important step in building the coachee's motivation.

Often the goal of a coaching engagement is to help the coachee to adapt his or her behaviors to achieve new goals. One example might be the classic extrovert who learns to take a breath, ask questions, and listen rather than steamrolling over his or her more introverted counterparts.

The coach must be able to create reflective and action-based, on-the-job learning experiences for the coachee to identify opportunities for applying emotional intelligence or critical thinking skills. The coach may need to educate the coachee in tools and techniques to apply on the job. And, the coach must create a process for evaluating the coachee's success and build accountability for continued application of the new skill.

This brings us to the important role of the coach in understanding which behaviors and drivers of behavior play to the coachee's strengths and which are getting in the way of success. It is imperative for the coach and coachee to gain awareness of what traits and beliefs come so naturally to the coachee that they must be a strong part of his or her daily life and an integral part of the coachee's feeling energized and fulfilled. A job may require a particular competency that is driven by a set of personality traits. But if this competency doesn't come naturally to the coachee, the job may always seem like an unnatural fit. Neurological findings reported by Kahneman (2011) support the conclusion that the more effort required to perform a task, the less energy is available to complete it. Even if a coachee learns to perform competently, he or she may not be satisfied by the job and may have difficulty maintaining a high level of performance

Knowing one's assets can be both a means of leveraging success as well as avoiding pitfalls. People have more energy and passion for activities that come naturally to them. Being aware of assets allows a coachee to use them constructively. They require less effort and guide us toward situations where we can be more successful. Early in my career, I was involved in joint projects with colleagues and found it difficult to complete many of them to my satisfaction. What I later learned is that my assets were more in the ideational and methodological stage of projects and less in the activities required for their completion. Once I realized this, I learned to work with colleagues who were strong finishers to complement my assets. My productivity improved, and I was much happier with the results.

The following case illustrates how an understanding of assets and liabilities helped a coachee to make a wise career choice.

Case Study: Managing Isn't for Everyone

Matt was a sociable and energetic individual. He enjoyed talking with people and was goal-oriented. This led to his considerable success as a sales representative for a food manufacturer. He was promoted to sales manager, but within a few months he began to fail. Shortly after his first year in the new role, Matt was terminated. Matt sought out a career coach to help him secure a new position as a sales manager.

The coach administered the Workplace Big Five Profile, which illustrates how "energizing," or enhancing the motivation of an individual, may enhance numerous job-related competencies. Matt was shocked to see that his personality was not a good fit for many of the business management competencies required of his promotion: leadership, decision-making, hiring talent, teamwork, and cooperation. However, the assessment predicted that Matt would be energized by one important competency: sales.

After discussing his past successes and failures with his coach, Matt realized that his personal satisfaction was greatest when he was working as an individual sales contributor. He found the tasks associated with management to be mentally and physically draining for him. Not only was he not a good performer in a management role, but he didn't feel he was achieving his life goals or using his strengths to their fullest extent. Matt landed a new job as a sales representative and quickly achieved top sales producer status.

This chapter has demonstrated how assessments can be useful in gaining insights about the assets and liabilities of the coachee. Assessments offer a rich reservoir of information about underlying abilities, values, and personality characteristics that influence behavior and actions. A skilled coach can use assessments as hypotheses toward a deeper understanding of a coachee's behavior. Chapter 4 will discuss the use of 360-degree feedback as a source of information about the coachee. The chapter will also address many of the most common questions asked about assessments, including their validity, how to select the right assessment and provider, and confidentiality.

Chapter 4: Additional Uses and Applications of Assessments in Coaching[3]

"He who knows others is learned; he who knows himself is wise."

Lao Tzu

Measuring Performance Using 360-Degree Feedback

So far, a variety of types of assessments have been shown to predict one's performance on the job. But, just because someone has the potential to be successful in a particular behavioral area, it doesn't necessarily mean that he or she is effectively using those talents. It is crucial in the coaching process to identify actual performance levels of the coachee, in addition to the potential measured by the self-assessment tools described in the previous chapter. Measuring the combination of potential and measured success provides critical information to the coach to determine not only where change is required but also the potential for change.

The most logical place to start is with the coachee's last formal performance review. Coaches might find documented areas of strength, as well as areas for improvement. However, this is not always a reliable process. Employer's performance review forms don't always measure the competencies and behaviors most

---

[3] This chapter is adapted from Pearl, Amy; Sharon Randaccio; and Alan G. Weinstein, 2010, *Using Assessment Tools to Enhance the Coaching Process*, an unpublished manuscript.

essential for an individual's particular position. In addition, they are often poorly administered, and, for a variety of reasons, the reviewing manager may or may not be honest and candid with the individual whose performance is being reviewed.

A better alternative is to utilize a formal 360-degree feedback assessment. Simply stated, 360-degree feedback is a powerful way to provide a deeper understanding of strengths, growth areas, and potential liabilities in order to enhance the development process. As part of a 360-degree assessment, coachees evaluate their own performance. In addition, managers, peers, direct reports, customers, vendors, or other raters complete the assessment. The result is a comprehensive and diverse picture of the perceptions of those individuals who work most closely with the coachee.

Collecting information from a variety of people with different perspectives increases the objectivity and validity of a feedback experience and provides richer, more specific information for the coachee.

Individual buy-in to the coaching process also increases, generating commitment from the coachee to personal development and increasing the likelihood of improved performance. The feedback from a 360-degree assessment accelerates change in performance by:

1. Providing multi-level feedback, identifying gaps in perceived performance.

2. Clearly defining skills and behavioral expectations.

3. Guiding participants to identify top strengths and growth areas.

4. Delivering actionable recommendations and development ideas.

5. Establishing a framework for development planning and measurement.

6. Creating a support team among managers, peers, and direct reports.

Vendors of 360-degree assessment programs provide suggested competency models but often offer models that can be customized to address specific competency areas and questions. Some surveys include both desirable and undesirable factors to gain a better understanding of potential liabilities. Many 360-degree feedback reports come with actionable ideas for building skills in each competency area and present feedback in simple, graphical, and easy to interpret formats.

Many coaches utilize an interview process to obtain 360-degree feedback. A written tool can supplement or replace that process with an objective, efficient, and consistent means of collecting and reporting information. A follow-up 360-degree assessment 12 to 18 months after the coaching process has been initiated can measure improvement and build accountability for behavioral change.

Case Study: The Rude Awaking

Laura, the leader of a clinical research unit within a life sciences company, was experiencing significant turnover in her division. Using assessments, the coach illustrated:

- *Laura's personality revealed her introverted nature, a high need for control, a high level of negative emotionality, and a skeptical perspective.*

- *Her emotional intelligence levels were only slightly below average. However, given the high level of EQ of her peers, her slightly below-average EQ scores were very problematic.*

- *Her critical thinking scores were extremely high, and she had been known as a brilliant scientist.*

Laura questioned the validity of the assessments and refused to believe that the turnover in her division was a result of her behaviors. She agreed to participate in a 360-degree assessment program to obtain objective feedback from her manager, direct reports, peers, and others with whom she worked. The results were devastating to Laura. She didn't realize she was perceived as someone who didn't share her knowledge with others, nor did she recognize that she often came across as aloof and non-

communicative. Laura was shocked that her behavior was negatively impacting almost everyone around her.

Confronted with the data, she began to look for solutions. Laura's pride would not allow her to fail in this process, so she spent over a year working with her coach. The coach helped Laura to:

- *Leverage her immense scientific knowledge by sharing this insight with her staff to broaden their knowledge, build team strength, and enhance their engagement.*
- *Set clear expectations with her team, delegate effectively, measure progress, and hold weekly team meetings to balance control with empowerment.*
- *Instead of being critical of others, establish a fact-finding process to use her critical thinking skills in a way that seemed less like criticism and more like probing questions.*

Laura made progress as demonstrated by a follow up 360-degree assessment that was administered a year later to assess progress in her key development areas. The coach then worked closely with Laura's manager to provide him with the necessary tools and techniques to continue the coaching process after the formal coaching engagement was completed.

Selecting the Right Assessments and Providers

Those who have decided to supplement their coaching process with assessment tools will find it essential to make a thorough evaluation of the tools and providers available. The following are some of the most important considerations that must be weighed.

Addressing the Question of Validity: Will the selected assessment tool help measure the characteristics that are important for your coaching engagements? Is the chosen tool reliable, in that the results it yields are reproducible and consistent? Are there benchmarks and normative data against which individual scores can be interpreted? What combination of tools will measure what you are trying to accomplish?

These questions are often addressed through the concept of *validity*. The validity of an assessment tool is usually measured by a statistical analysis of the relationship between the given tool and some behavioral or outcome criteria. Although significant research backs the industry's leading tools, some assessments do not lend themselves to traditional scrutiny of their validity because the assessment characteristics are not independent.

Herbert Simon, a Nobel laureate, suggested using a "heuristic" approach to problem-solving, one based on experience and common sense when hypotheses cannot be validated in other ways (Simon 1973). This can be a useful approach to explaining the validation and application of assessments. A good assessment tool is one that generates hypotheses that can be investigated using information from other assessments or observations. A skilled coach uses his or her common sense and experience to build a conceptual map, integrating the tendencies identified through assessments and discussions with the coachee.

For example, a person who profiles as a strong "Conscientiousness/Cautious" in DiSC may also profile as high in "Consolidation" in the Workplace Big Five. This coachee may demonstrate behaviors such as detail orientation, methodicalness, analytical thinking, and risk aversion. Using multiple assessments offers stronger support upon which reasonable predictions can be made about a coachee's behavior. Coaching discussions should reveal behaviors that are consistent with these predictions. While building the coachee's personal balance sheet, using multiple assessments and observations of behavior will enhance the validity of the assessment information.

Choosing an Assessment Provider: A coach does not need to be an assessment research expert. Rather, the coach needs to select an assessment provider that supports his or her needs and coaching approach.

First, consider whether the assessment firm is an assessment publisher, consultancy, or software company. Each will provide different levels of academic/research or organizational development expertise. The coach's own knowledge base and experience will dictate the type of information and support needed from the assessment provider.

Second, consider the level of customer support offered by the provider. Does the training offered initially and on an on-going basis meet your needs? What costs are involved with on-going support? Can the provider offer insights to help you review assessment results, interpretations, and programs for your clients? Are training and coaching materials supplied so that the results can actually be of use to you?

Legal Compliance: Does the tool comply with industry guidelines and with employment legislation? The U. S. Department of Labor has specific guidelines for utilizing assessments to support hiring decisions. Although these restrictions seldom impact coaching engagements, it is important to realize that many coachees embrace the assessment process and have a desire to learn more about their existing team members and job candidates. The coachee may wish to utilize the same assessments he or she experienced in the coaching process when considering potential new hires. A coach should be knowledgeable about a tool's application before recommending multiple uses.

User Requirements: Does the tool require that you be trained or certified in some way? Based on a commitment to accurate and ethical assessments of individuals, providers use qualification systems to help ensure the right tools are in the right hands. The most sophisticated tools require a high level of expertise in test interpretation and, therefore, require licensure or certification to practice in your state in a field related to the assessment tool. Some even require a doctorate degree in psychology, education, or a closely related field with evidence of formal training in psychometric tools. Others have no special qualifications for purchase and may require a simple certification class to be able to administer the tools. Effective coaches tap into the training and support provided by the vendors and also network with other certified consultants to broaden their knowledge, develop their coaching skills, and ensure they are using the tools in the most effective manner. Note that it may be a poor use of talent or time for some coaches to become licensed, when their own strengths lend themselves to spending quality time with clients. These coaches may choose to partner with certified professionals to administer assessments, interpret their results, and, potentially, debrief their coachees in order to enhance the usefulness of assessments in the coaching process.

Some FAQs about Application of Assessments in Coaching

This section will provide answers to some frequently asked questions regarding the application of assessments in the coaching process.

Q: Are assessments tests?

A: Care has been taken in this chapter to utilize the words "assessments" or "tools" rather than the word "test." The term "test" implies that there are right and wrong answers being generated by an assessment—which is clearly not the case. Assessments are a way of understanding how we think and learn and why we each think and learn differently. The most effective assessment tools will produce a profile for the coach and coachee to use in deciding whether the coachee's profile fits the expectations and the culture of his or her organization and whether the coachee is fully utilizing his or her strengths.

However, use caution here. Many of the most popular assessments are completely non-judgmental and convey the message that "we're all okay, just different." The publishers of such assessment models claim there is no such thing as a bad profile, just different types of people. It is then up to the professional judgment of the coach to recognize that, even though there may be no "right" answer, some individuals will be more capable of meeting the demands of a particular position or organizational culture based on the strengths inherent in their personal profile. The essence of coaching is helping the coachee to find alignment between personal strengths and career fit. That goal cannot be met through an assessment alone; instead, meeting it requires the professional administration of the assessment as one part of a comprehensive coaching strategy.

Q: Do assessments focus on weaknesses?

A: The best tools guide coachees to discover their strengths, their beliefs, and their liabilities. In some cases, it is the coachee's defined strength that gets in the way when overused or applied in the wrong situation. For example, the conscientious, detail-oriented individual can become paralyzed by the analysis associated with decision-making. Such an individual, who has a talent for reducing risk and finding the optimal outcome, can become derailed by this trait if he or she becomes mired in the need to make a perfect decision. Learning how to apply strengths more appropriately in those situations would be a desired coaching outcome.

It is important in the coaching process to use the assessment results as a contributor to the full balance sheet. What are the coachee's assets, and how can he or she use them more effectively? What are the coachee's liabilities, how important are they to success in this role, and, if critical, how does he or she develop the skills necessary to limit them?

Q: Do assessments tell you whether a person is right for a job?

A: Assessments alone will not tell an employer if a person is right for a job. But, the more information and understanding the employer has, the more likely he or she will be able to predict success in a particular job in a particular company. No single assessment tool exists that measures this at the 100 percent probability level. However, using the right assessment tools in combination with effective interviewing techniques will increase the probability of drawing correct insights.

Q: Who gets to see the assessment results?

A: Assessment results are personal and sensitive. However, the people surrounding the coachee cannot contribute to the success of the coaching engagement if they don't have open discussions about behaviors and other attributes of the coachee. Therefore, it is recommended, with permission of the coachee, that data be shared, but always in a sensitive and thoughtful way.

When assessment results are received, they should be reviewed in a one-on-one meeting between the coach and coachee. The coachee should be given an opportunity to study the results in detail and to ask clarifying questions about the assessment model and results. Once the coachee is clear on the meaning and value— as well as any limitations—of the assessment results, the coach and coachee should create a development plan that will best achieve the objectives of the coaching engagement based on the coachee's assessment profile.

Once the plan is developed, the coach should facilitate a meeting with the coachee and his or her manager to review the assessment results at a level of detail with which the coachee feels comfortable. It is ultimately the manager's responsibility to mentor and coach the coachee over the long-term, so the assessment results can be beneficial. However, too much detail can be overwhelming and can detract from the coachee's development plan. It is not important that the manager know every detail about the assessment results, unless he or she is going to use the information for the benefit of the coachee. Most importantly, the manager needs to understand general themes and future action steps of the coaching program.

The coachee's manager and/or direct reports should also consider taking the same assessments. Having an open discussion comparing the coachee's profile to the profiles of co-workers can expedite efforts to identify opportunities to enhance relationships and achieve better results. And the ability to share the results of a common process and terminology will help ensure a more consistent application of goals.

Many organizations maintain assessment results in their human resources department. If this is the case, the coach should ensure that the in-house human resources professionals who may be viewing or using the results of the assessment are educated in the models, the assessment process, and the interpretation and use of the results.

Q: *As a coach, how can you benefit from taking the assessments yourself?*

A: The simple answer is that you can't effectively use assessment tools with your coachees until you really understand yourself and your coaching style. Using assessments personally will provide you with insight into how to approach the change process with your coachee. It will also give you an effective way to practice interpreting results for someone you know best: *you.*

Conclusions

Chapters 3 and 4 have attempted to provide a thorough overview of the considerations and approaches associated with integrating assessments into the coaching process. In short, assessments may offer valid, reliable, and user-friendly tools to create stronger dialogue between the coach and coachee. Assessments allow an individual to look into the mirror, build self-awareness, and create a balance sheet of personal assets and liabilities. Assessment tools also help a coachee to understand his or her supervisors, direct reports, peers, spouses, life partners, and others around them in order to create more meaningful and productive relationships.

Although there are many assessment tools on the market today, a coach should take the time to research and find tools that support his or her coaching philosophy and client needs. Maintaining knowledge of current research, approaches, and trends in this area can enhance the coach's ability to support the needs of his or her coachees.

Chapter 5: Coaching through Reflection

"You get the best effort from others not by lighting a fire beneath them but by building a fire within."

Bob Nelson

The Old Coaching Paradigm

Traditional approaches to developing executives have mostly included off-site programs designed to enlighten the executive and broaden his or her skill-set as well as direct meetings with the executive's manager. Until recently, executive coaching conducted by an inside or outside professional was rare. When an executive needed to change, he or she was typically sent to a program that focused on the perceived area that needed changing, or "fixing". Top executive prospects were often sent to elite university programs for several weeks to learn new skills that would prepare them for top jobs. Others were sent to shorter programs for a crash course in leadership, a business specialty, or other skill. Still others were sent to remedial programs designed to correct a weakness. For the most part, all of these programs had limited effectiveness in changing people. Much of what was learned in them was out of context and rarely gained traction when the executive returned to the company.

MBA programs have become very popular today as a means of developing executive skills. These programs are often seen as a

88

stepping stone to a high-ranking executive position. However, a growing body of research is indicating the failure of these programs to teach skills relevant to the effectiveness of future company leaders. The students who complete these programs are often left with the nearly insurmountable task of applying complex academic concepts and analytical tools to company challenges, a task that most of their teachers would struggle with. Clearly, a disconnect exists between what is being taught in MBA programs and the challenges that MBA students experience in their companies. While earning an MBA can add real value in exposing students to a broad range of important business topics and skills, it is not a leadership-enhancing experience.

A similar disconnect often exists in training programs offered within organizations. Internal programs designed to inculcate skills or new leadership methods typically have a short life span if not immediately applied. Much is lost in the failure to implement what is learned in these programs, leaving the trainee wondering why the company is spending money for training with so little return on its investment. The cynicism felt by employees attending these programs is often ignored by those who sponsor them. It is not unusual for participants to attend, knowing that little will change as a result of their participation because the follow-up implementation of change rarely happens.

The internal methods employed by most companies to create executive change include direct confrontation, consultation, training, and developmental workshops. Most companies use some form of performance management system to rate or rank an executive as a means of providing feedback and identifying gaps in his or her behavior and/or performance. Many company leaders lack the skills to coach, often choosing less-than-effective methods of dealing with underachievers. In the case of an executive who needs to make changes, the feedback he or she receives is often vague and lacking specific details of changes needed. Moreover, the feedback may also be presented in a direct and confrontational manner, which can lead to defensiveness or resistance by the recipient. But the most crucial ingredient—and the one most often missing from the majority of corporate performance-management systems—is feedback or guidance on the changes needed for success. Negative feedback focused on identifying faults or weaknesses fails to offer its recipient guidelines for change—let alone any recognition of strengths that might form the foundation for growth.

In summary, traditional methods of developing executives have failed for several reasons. In the case of educational programs such as the MBA, their value is primarily to broaden the executive and expose him or her to many business topics. The MBA is not designed to develop leaders. The internal corporate programs designed to teach skills often fall short of expectations because of the disconnect between what is learned and what is applied to the operations of the company. Much is forgotten before it is useful.

Most approaches to executive development are primarily designed to correct a fault. They were not designed to develop or to help the executive identify and leverage his or her strengths. Executive development approaches also tend to use criticism and negative feedback, which can demoralize its recipient. As stated earlier, executives generally lack the skills necessary for them to develop their successors.

The New Coaching Paradigm

One reason that executive coaching has become popular is that it addresses—and remedies—the failures of traditional executive development. Coaching begins with a psychological contract to change what the coach and coachee agree is important to the success of the coachee. Coaching is centered on the coachee, not the coach. The coach acts as a catalyst for change. While the coach is involved in the process, it is the coachee who needs to do the "heavy lifting."

As discussed in Chapter 2, many coaches do not make a distinction between coaching and consulting. These coaches tend to give advice under the guise of coaching. While this advice may be helpful, effective coaching creates a learning environment in which the coach asks probing questions and explores the coachee's past and present experiences. This movement away from advising and toward questioning shifts the focus clearly onto the coachee and provides information that is critically relevant to the ultimate success of the coaching experience. The responsibility for dialogue rests with the coachee, not the coach. Inasmuch as this dialogue will guide the coach's queries, which, in turn, will lead to insights on what is really going on in the thinking and behavior of the coachee, full and uninhibited dialogue is a necessary component of any successful coaching relationship.

Reflection

Reflection is a powerful method of recreating past experiences. By recalling experiences, the coachee recreates situations that offer clues about how the coachee thought and acted at the time the situation occurred. An example might help illustrate this point.

One of my coachees reflected on a situation that occurred when one of his employees failed to meet a deadline on an important project. The situation turned tense, and my coachee became angry, condescending, and demeaning toward this employee. He later learned that the missed deadline was due to circumstances outside the employee's control. One of the coachee's goals was to be approachable and fair with his management team. By recounting this experience, he was able to reflect not only on what he did wrong but also to consider other behaviors that would have been more fruitful in understanding the reasons for the missed deadline and preventing his reaction from reoccurring in the future. Reflection allowed my coachee to realize he had missed not only the opportunity to solve a problem but had also fallen far short of his personal goal of being approachable. We next turned our attention to how he was going to reestablish his positive rapport with this employee.

Some additional questions that helped in this case and will always help the coachee reframe reflected experience are, "What could I have done differently that would bring me closer to a desirable outcome? What mistakes could I have avoided by choosing a different approach? What did I learn from this reflection and analysis?"

Reflective coaching does not stop at recalling and analyzing past experiences. It also seeks to model desirable behavioral patterns and report successes and failures of the desired model in coaching sessions. Change requires reframing behavior and practicing new behaviors. It is one thing to reframe a situation in a coaching session but quite another to apply the new approach or behavior in new situations in real time.

Using reflection as a coaching method has its challenges. Some coachees have difficulty expressing their reflected experience. They may not be able to remember the details. Or, they may have difficulty relating their current experiences to past reflections—an approach that can sometimes identify the origin of a behavioral pattern through reflecting on the past. A skilled coach must help the coachee reconstruct experiences through deft questioning. Many times, the reflected experience being shared by the coachee may seem to be stalled or difficult to recount, often with the coachee showing emotion or tension when responding. This is a clue to the coach that he or she must probe more deeply.

Reflective learning as a method of coaching can be broken down into seven stages, as follows:

Seven Stages of Reflection

1. **Historical: think of a time when you...**
    a. tried to lead
    b. were a team member
    c. failed
    d. succeeded

2. **Describe your experience:**
    a. Who was there?
    b. What happened?
    c. What were the consequences?

3. **Frame the experience with an alternative approach or behavior designed to improve the outcome**
    a. Choose an approach that fits
    b. Try the new approach out for a test run

4.   **Analyze the experience using the new approach as a framework**

5.   **What conclusions can you draw from applying the new approach?**

   a.   What insight did you gain?

   b.   Did it help you understand what happened?

   c.   If it did not help you understand what happened, why not?

6.   **Apply the same approach to a current challenge or opportunity**

   a.   What insight do you hope to gain?

   b.   Will it help you understand what is happening?

   c.   Will it not help you understand what is happening?

7.   **Write and document your experience, analysis, and application of your new approach**

Case Study: The Seven Stages of Reflection in Team Building

Bob was an aspiring executive in his family business. He was struggling to develop his department into a cohesive unit. When asked to reflect on previous experiences with teams, he recalled his experiences playing basketball. He had been a college star basketball player and spent two years in Europe playing professional basketball. His experience in Europe left him discouraged about team play. His team was dysfunctional and never jelled as a unit. The result was a poor record and a bad experience. When he described what happened, he related that the team was made up of players from different countries, speaking different languages. The consequence of this heterogeneous group was poor communication and every player working independently on his own agenda.

We talked about what could have helped the team, and he came up with several suggestions, such as team meetings, interpreters to help overcome language barriers, stronger emphasis on team play, and better preparation for rival teams. All suggestions were aimed at investing time and energy into communicating, collaborating, and cooperating within the team. Using these suggestions, he began to see how things may have been different if this approach had been applied to his basketball team. This insight helped him to develop a new approach to his current work team. At our next meeting, he articulated how he applied this new approach and the initial positive reception he received from team members. In a few weeks, he reported a major breakthrough in aligning his team toward group goals.

The insights gained from reflection can be powerful. Followed by reframing, which will be discussed in detail in the next section, the coachee is now able to test new behaviors. Through practice and continued reflection with a coach, newly learned behaviors can be established and replace old behaviors that were less effective. It is important for the coachee to recognize his or her progress by the coach continually asking whether the new behavior is making a difference. Recognizing and acknowledging progress is rewarding and will serve to reinforce change. This progress should be documented and kept on record to support evidence of change.

In summary, reflection works in coaching by articulating the coachee's experiences, both past and present. The coach will need to ask probing questions to help the coachee gain a deeper understanding of the experience. Reframing the experience is crucial to the application of new and more effective behaviors. Finally, applying the new behavior to new situations, along with continued feedback about its effectiveness, will increase the likelihood that the change will be reinforced and sustainable.

Why is reflection such an important methodology in coaching? There are several reasons why. Reflection is based in reality. This makes it immediately relevant to the person who is reflecting on his or her experiences. Relevance personalizes the coaching process, which leads to a stronger connection between coaching and change. Reflection also lends itself to analysis and a deeper understanding of behavior. This, in turn, leads to a greater opportunity to identify alternative behaviors that may move the coachee closer to his or her goal. By identifying a desirable alternative response to a reflected situation, the coachee is able to test it out in new situations and receive continuous feedback on its effectiveness. This feedback should be part of the ongoing dialogue between coach and coachee.

From a coach's perspective, this is a win/win strategy. With reflection, there is a shift in who does most of the talking in a coaching relationship and who owns the insights leading to change. This is motivating to both parties. For the coach, satisfaction with any coaching relationship is directly correlated to the coachee taking full responsibility for change. This allows the coach to concentrate on the coaching process, listening to what is being said and responding with thoughtful questions that will promote insight into the thought process of the coachee.

Reflection almost always leads to insight, but insight does not always lead to change. As much as we may each desire change, habitual behaviors steeped in years of practice can be very resistant to change. Below are three approaches that will improve the chances of change through coaching.

Reframing

Reframing is the process of changing the lens through which a situation is viewed. In my experience in working with CEOs and other senior managers, the challenge they bring forth is often obscured by their biases. For example, a coachee felt his brother, who had entered the company 10 years after he did, was competing with him for majority control of stock ownership. This coachee believed he was the rightful majority owner because of his seniority and CEO leadership. He was building resentment toward his brother, and this bothered him. His brother ran a smaller department that was struggling. Guided by probing questions, the coachee revealed to his coach that the real challenge had been created by their father, who was trying to help his younger son by gifting him additional stock in the company. The father's rationale was to treat each son equally, and the gift of stock was simply intended as a compensation for the younger son's lack of seniority and leadership role within the company. The approach to dealing with the father was very different than with the brother. By reframing the situation, the coachee was able to approach his brother with his concerns. It turned out the brother was not interested in owning more stock in the company. The two brothers subsequently approached the father to offer their different goals, greatly reducing the tension that was building between the brothers.

In the case described above, the coach was able to help the coachee view his concern by asking clarifying and probing questions. This is one approach to reframing, called "conceptual reframing." The goal of conceptual reframing is to change the lens that the coachee uses to interpret the challenge brought forth. This, in turn, will lead to alternative approaches to resolve the situation. The coach can then help by identifying the new tension that will lead to action and eventual change.

Another approach to reframing is to reinterpret a situation using an asset. One of my coaching clients received critical feedback from his CEO for not developing his team members better. As COO, he was expected to be grooming his people for career advancement. His assessments indicated that he was very task-oriented and was challenged when dealing with the so-called "softer side" of managing people. The assessments also showed strong assets centered around responsibility and achievement. By reinterpreting his liability in not developing his people as a goal to be achieved, he was able to create a developmental plan with each individual on his team. Thus, he used an asset of achievement to reframe a liability—and with great success. This was quickly recognized by his CEO, and he was congratulated on his progress. In reflecting on his own change, the COO was surprised at how easy it was to change his own behavior once he was able to rely on his existing strengths to achieve his results.

An important goal in coaching is to always seek ways to leverage assets and manage liabilities. But what if an executive role calls for assets that the incumbent in that role does not have?

This was the case for a CEO whose strengths were strategic thinking, a focus on the future, an engaging personality, and a strong external network of contacts. However, when it came to details and holding people accountable, he would readily admit to failure. As the founder of the company, he was able to grow it through networking and a strategy of producing high-quality products and providing strong customer care. However, as his company grew in size, he was not paying enough attention to the lack of accountability and leadership that had begun to create a dysfunctional culture. When exploring his assets that were fueling the company's growth and his liabilities that were limiting the internal organization, it became obvious to him that he needed an internal partner. He searched for an executive whose assets complemented his liabilities. The plan was to make this new executive the general manager, with the authority to run the day-to-day transactions of the company.

The result was continued growth of the company, a much improved organizational culture, and a happy CEO/owner who was now able to leverage his own assets more effectively. One outcome of this organizational partnership was the challenge of having two executives very different from one another working together very closely. This is an ongoing challenge in this case. Yet both parties realize how beneficial their complementary assets are to overall company success. With the help of coaching, the CEO has reframed this relationship as critical to his need to grow his company. He meets regularly with his general manager to coordinate plans and to resolve any conflicts resulting from their differences.

Chapter 2 emphasized the importance of tension in creating change. Reflective coaching only works when there is tension. While tension drives the process of change, it does not give direction to change.

A recent coachee was confronted with a dilemma at work. His raise for the following year was lower than expected and lower than several other executives who had less seniority, lower positions in the company, and unproven productivity. Even with the potential to earn a performance-based bonus, his disappointing raise did not sit well with him. Coaching revealed that the feedback he received from his manager was twofold. First, his performance over the past three years was below expectations. Second, he was perceived as having a weaker work ethic than his peers, as evidenced by his hours in the office and amount of business-related travel. The tension was strong. He was upset and questioning his future in the company, but the approach he would take to relieve the tension was not clear. The company did not want him to leave, but they also wanted to deliver the message that they were not happy with his performance. Coaching helped him to explore his options. As he reflected on his strong desire to succeed in his current job, the dialogue shifted from his frustration toward how he would become more productive in the eyes of those who evaluated him. The direction of his effort became clear as he examined his needs. He stepped up his effort and is making progress toward a productive year. While he still feels he was treated unfairly, his tension shifted away from resentment and toward the challenge of proving his manager wrong about his value to the company.

In summary, reframing can be a powerful coaching method of changing behavior and can usually be categorized in one of three ways. First, conceptual reframing works through the coach asking clarifying and probing questions to get at the real challenge faced by the coachee. Second, helping a coachee in leveraging an asset to overcome a liability will help change to occur more naturally. The third reframing approach encourages a coachee to partner or work with someone who has complementary assets to his or her liabilities. In all cases, the inevitable tension created by the need for change must find direction. By staying focused on the desired outcome or goal, the coach and coachee will ensure that tension resolves itself successfully.

Chapter 6: Common Challenges in Executive Coaching

"Leadership is helping other people grow and succeed.
Leadership is not just about you; it's about them."
Jack Welch

Coaching is not just about closing gaps and creating tension. Gaps exist for many reasons, and tension is an inevitable byproduct of the growth process, but an executive coach must be aware of both. This chapter explores five challenges that contribute to the gaps between effective leadership and underperformance. These challenges serve as examples of the conceptual richness that a coach must have to engage the coachee in the change process. The last section in this chapter describes ways of acquiring and supporting coaching skills.

Control

Most of the coaching clients I have worked with had a strong need to control their workplace and their people. This should not be surprising. Successful executives learn to rely on themselves as the best way they know to accomplish goals and reduce the chances of failure. This is a mixed blessing. While it is true that success can be realized through control, it can also be inhibited by control. Executives tend to be very busy, often overwhelmed by their roles. Trying to maintain control over all aspects of work can handicap an executive by limiting the time and concentration needed to lead a complex organization. The greater the complexity, the greater the cost in time and focus to maintain control.

Why do executives hold on to control? There are many reasons. One reason is lack of trust. Why should an executive risk failure by counting on others who are either not as driven to succeed or not as skilled? Self-reliance is built on a philosophy of personal self-confidence. This attribution does not easily extend to others. We trust ourselves and are confident of our own capabilities; therefore, we hold onto the reins of decision-making and authority and rely only on ourselves.

Control is also appealing to executives because of fear. It is always a leap of faith to rely on others who might disappoint you. This fear holds us back from involving others and may even undermine the motivation of others who would work with us. Fear is a strong motivator and difficult to overcome. Controlling out of fear may also create situations leading others to fear the leader.

Still another reason executives cling to control is they really do not have the available talent with whom they trust to share control. Executives often inherit staff and a set of organizational norms that may prevent them from creating a high-functioning team to support them. Organizations that do not hire top talent or do not invest in developing their associates may be encouraging executives to hold on to control.

Whatever the reason, executives who maintain control have a tendency to micro-manage. This leads to a self-fulfilling prophecy: by controlling work, an executive prevents his or her associates from engaging in challenging work and, at the same time, limits associate opportunities to grow into more responsible roles. Lack of opportunity for associates to learn and grow will reinforce their self-perception as unqualified for responsibility and therefore in need of control by executives. This scenario is a fertile area for remediation by executive coaching.

Delegation

A concept related to control, delegation is a strategy to engage others in taking over both responsibility and authority. Executives who delegate successfully are able to take on more work. They are also able to lead at a higher level, overseeing projects without micro-managing the associates assigned to them. Effective delegation frees executives to explore strategic initiatives without being saddled with the activities that are performed by associates. As discussed more fully in Chapter 7, the higher an executive ascends within an organization, the more strategic and less tactical he or she should become. From a coaching perspective, effective delegation will help manage workflow and develop personnel. Gaps in workflow management can be a fertile area to address problems with delegation and associate development.

106

While there is little doubt effective delegation is key to executive success, many executives fail at it. Clearly, the need to control is one reason, but another significant reason is lack of understanding of how to delegate. Dumping activities and assigning tasks is not an effective way of delegating. Unless there is a process that promotes both responsibility and the authority to be engaged in work, delegation loses its motivational appeal to associates. In her book on delegation, *If You Want It Done Right, You Don't Have To Do It Yourself!*, Donna Genett (2004) describes the delegation process to include preparation, clarity of expected assignment, explicit timeframe, level of authority, and frequent follow-up and feedback. She also suggests a debriefing with associates to review what went well and what needed improvement after the delegated assignment is completed. This process is designed to allow executives to develop associates while staying fully informed about the delegated assignment.

Because successful delegation requires a lot of work, many executives will lack the motivation to engage in this process. The coach's role is to point out the gaps that exist, at least in part, because of the failure to delegate. These gaps may include the failure to develop associates to grow into a greater role within an organization, a lack of time to concentrate on strategic initiatives, and a lack of progress in creating a positive organizational culture. The goal for the coach is both to acknowledge the effort that goes into delegation and to allow executives to see the cost/benefit advantages to engaging in it.

A lack of trust in associates will limit delegation. As mentioned earlier, this may be due to the executive having a problem letting go. It may also be attributable to a real or perceived lack of talent among associates. In either case, the executive who lacks trust will engage in less delegation—which, in turn, will reduce his or her effectiveness. This is a very difficult obstacle to overcome. Failure to let go of work can be deeply ingrained into the personality of the executive. Lack of talent may be endemic in an organization because of low pay scales, a poor associate selection process, or a failure to create and use a performance management system that ensures professional development and high-quality performers. Coaches will need to explore all of these possibilities and maintain tension on those in need of change.

Communication

Communication needs to be addressed both for its content and context (the content of communication has already been discussed in Chapters 2 and 5). The major content issues relate to creating gaps and tension through information acquired from assessments and coaching sessions and then asking probing questions that help the coach to create enough tension to motivate the coachee to action that will reduce the tension.

The context of communication is very complex. I will focus on a few of the more important context factors that impact communication in coaching. These factors fall under four topics: establishing rapport, being in the moment, active listening, and reflective learning.

Rapport. For coaching to be effective, it is imperative to establish rapport. This involves demonstrating trust and confidentiality, a perceived respect for the coach by the coachee, and sensitivity by the coach to a very personal situation involving major consequences for the coachee. First impressions are important. My personal approach to establishing rapport is to be very transparent up front. I make it very clear what my role is as a coach. I talk about the goals of the coaching engagement, my approach to coaching, the coaching model I use, and the importance I place on confidentiality. I also address any concerns or questions the coachee may have. I pay particular attention to aligning the interests of the coachee with my interests as a coach.

Being in the Moment. This is one of the most difficult skills to learn as a coach. Being in the moment can sometimes feel like being unprepared. It seems natural to want to prepare questions for the coachee in advance and to anticipate areas of fertile coaching. Preparing questions, however, defeats the intuitive process needed for coaching to be successful. Coaches need to be active listeners and observers, identifying cues that signal tension and areas for deeper probing. They need to rely on their intuition to follow up on their hunches. Scripting questions in advance will be counterproductive. Remember, the coachee is the subject, not the coach. Coaches need to concentrate on what is going on emotionally and cognitively with the coachee.

Active Listening. Much has been written about active listening. The main lesson for coaching from the available research and clinical observations is that active listening is a process, beginning with readiness to paraphrase what the coachee is saying. Active listening will also signal to the coachee that you are in the moment. Rephrasing will provide an opportunity to verify and obtain feedback on your understanding of what was said, adding to the goal of clarity in communication. Active listening will aid the coach in identifying tensions and gaps that otherwise might go unnoticed.

Reflective Learning. Chapter 5 discussed reflective coaching in detail. Learning the skill of using reflection as a methodology of coaching is essential in examining the coachee's experiences and applying new ways of addressing them. This is where new learning can take place—not as an added lesson but as a reflective insight from the analysis of how the new learning can be applied to past situations with a higher likelihood of favorable results moving forward. By applying newly learned approaches to recalled experiences, the transfer of new learning will be enhanced. This is attributable to the immediate relevance and reinforcement of the new learning.

Reflected experiences should include both past and present situations that are relevant to positive change. Having the coachee apply the newly learned behavior to new situations will allow for practice and feedback, further reinforcing the efficacy of the new behavior. Coaches should encourage coachees to relate current experiences. These are live cases, relevant and ripe for analysis and fertile ground to try out new, more effective behaviors.

Personality Styles

Having assessment information will greatly enhance the understanding of personal style and personality characteristics of the coachee. Understanding individual differences and how they determine certain behaviors can help a coach to approach the coachee much more effectively. For example, if the DiSC indicates a very direct personal style with a backup style of cautiousness (DC), the coach's approach to the coachee can be more direct, identifying the tasks needed for change. On the other hand, if the coachee has a highly inspirational, persuasive style, the approach may be more conversational, allowing the coachee to self-analyze behavioral patterns This, in turn, will help the coachee to better understand how to use his or her style more effectively to obtain better results as a leader. For example, this coachee may try looking at all sides of an issue with associates with a goal of convincing them that one approach has more merit, and therefore, should be embraced.

Sometimes the personal style of the coach clashes with that of the coachee. For example, I have had difficulty with coachees who are categorized as "sensors" on the MBTI. Being an intuitive thinker, I often find it challenging when my coachee struggles with intuitive thinking, such as defining a vision. Sensors want data and concreteness, and that is often next to impossible for them to grasp when discussing vision, which is abstract and general. In this case, I would look for other ways to talk about vision with a sensor coachee, trying to be as concrete as I can. This can be difficult, given my behavioral style. Nevertheless, flexibility and adapting to the coachee's style will greatly enhance the coaching relationship.

Learning Styles

Another area that affects coaching is the way a coachee learns. Research suggests that people learn in three different modes: visual, auditory, and kinesthetic. Visual learners represent a significant percentage of all people and respond best to visual cues. In a coaching session, reflections can serve as visual cues because the situation can be recalled and the coachee can visualize what happened. Auditory learners respond well to dialogue. They are able to learn by listening. Again, reflections produce auditory cues as well as visual ones, providing a rich medium for learning. Kinesthetic, or "hands-on," learners need to actually *do* things to really understand them. They need to apply what they have learned and experience the verification that occurs through application of learning. Live cases, analysis, and application of newly acquired behaviors lend themselves well for kinesthetic learners. It is important for a coach to be aware of learning styles and tailor his or her approach to the coachee's learning style.

Body language can make the coachee more comfortable in what can be a stressful situation. For example, if a coachee is leaning forward, the coach may also do the same, not so much to mimic the coachee but to respond to him or her in a similar fashion. Reflecting the body language of the coachee may have a subliminal impact in making him or her more responsive. This use of reflective body language is similar to verbal paraphrasing, only with body movement rather than dialogue. The lasting impression and value it provides is that the coach is fully engaged and responding to the coachee throughout the coaching experience.

On Becoming a Coach

This section will explore ways to acquire coaching skills and discuss some of the most common resources for building one's coaching skills. Chapter 7 will address the importance of the business knowledge an executive coach needs to have in order to be effective in coaching high-level executives.

Academic Programs: Where and how does a person learn to become a successful executive coach? There are very few academic programs teaching coaching skills. Only a scattering of MBA courses in executive coaching have been created and taught. According to much of the coaching literature, most executive coaches do not have formal training or a certification in coaching. A non-profit association of personal and executive business coaches, the International Coach Federation (ICF; www.coachfederation.org), seeks to promote the professional development of coaches and preserve the integrity of the coaching profession. ICF supports development of individuals working in the coaching profession and sponsors programs to maintain professional standards within the field. ICF has local chapters in major metropolitan areas that promote its coaching programs. Two other certification organizations that promote coaching standards are the International Association of Coaching (IAC; www.certifiedcoach.org) and Coaches Training Institute (CTI; www.coachestraininginstitute.org).

While academic institutions rarely offer courses in coaching, there are institutes dedicated to teaching coaching skills. For example, the Fielding Institute, in Santa Barbara, California, offers courses that will prepare professional coaches. There are other certification programs that require many hours of supervised experience with a master coach in order to be accredited as a coach. Several Gestalt institutions, like the Gestalt Institute of

Cleveland, in Cleveland, Ohio, help their students adopt a holistic approach to working with coaching clients. These programs profess to be rigorous, and they do require many hours of training. However, the verdict is still out on whether these programs truly prepare executive coaches who deeply understand the coaching process discussed in this book.

Online Programs: As in so many other areas today, coaching certification programs and coaching associations are becoming increasingly Internet-based. While these types of online programs are probably emerging to meet the growing demand for the services of the coaching profession, many experienced executive coaches have serious doubts about the efficacy of these online programs. As discussed in Chapter 1, a "one-size-fits-all" commodity approach to executive coaching is a recipe for disappointment. The coaching certification process should not be trivialized. An executive coaching certification program is an intensive, interpersonal development process requiring face-to-face mentoring from a master coach; it simply cannot be achieved over the Internet.

Reading: A great deal of knowledge about coaching can be acquired through reading. Dozens of books and articles have been written about coaching. However, the quality of these writings varies greatly. I have a personal bias toward coaching books that are based on a change model. After all, change is what coaching is supposed to accomplish. Readings that have change at their core are rare, but some noteworthy exceptions exist, such as these five, which are highly recommended: *Leading Change*, by John P. Kotter; *Deep Change* and *Building a Bridge as You Walk on It*, both by Robert E. Quinn; *Grow Your Own Leaders: How to Identify, Develop, and Retain Leadership Talent*, by William C. Byham, Audrey B. Smith and Matthew J. Paese; and *The Art and Practice of Leadership Coaching: 50 Top Executive Coaches Reveal Their Secrets*, edited by Howard Morgan, Phil Harkins, and Marshall Goldsmith. A sixth book recommended is a parable with an excellent example of a coach and a coachee as they experience the process of coaching (*Leading with Soul*, by Lee G. Bolman and Terrance E. Deal)

Coaching Groups: One way to learn more about coaching is through interacting with other executive coaches. In joining a coaching group, try to seek out coaches who really understand what coaching is all about. You could then meet with them to share knowledge as well as to support each other in advancing coaching as a profession. Several years ago, I founded a group of executive coaches who met monthly and explored different approaches to coaching. Some coaches went through Gestalt training; others worked on deep change techniques, using brain research as the basis for their approach to coachees. Still others were graduates of academic programs that taught courses in leadership, communication, and change. One was an experienced business executive who was self-taught as a coach. These varied backgrounds showed me that coaching is a dynamic and complex process. Being part of a professional network of colleagues who engage in effective executive coaching will enhance your continued learning about the coaching process.

For-Profit Programs: Companies have been founded to train coaches in their mission to teach executives how to be more effective. I have been associated with one such company for over 20 years. Vistage International (formerly TEC) recruits coaches and former top executives with a high aptitude for coaching to be chairs. Vistage trains its chairs to select CEOs and top executives to be members in groups of non-competing businesses. The purpose of these groups is to provide a forum for learning, group problem-solving, and individual coaching. Executives meet in monthly group sessions to learn about a variety of business topics from knowledge experts. They then reconvene in executive sessions to learn from each other. The chair facilitates a conversation between a member who has a challenge or opportunity, and the group at large. The result of this conversation is a clarification of the real issue and processing the issue with peers. After listening to the advice of other group members, the presenting member makes a commitment to the chair and the group to follow up on his or her issue and to report back to the group on progress. Between group meetings, the chair also engages in one-on-one coaching sessions with each member to follow up and help the executive stay focused on resolving the challenge or pursuing the opportunity presented. Some issues take months to get resolved, and the Vistage chair and group member continue to work on the issue until it is resolved. This process is designed to enhance the effectiveness of the executive, both in the group and through individual coaching.

Vistage training for chairs is very intense and utilizes many of the coaching methods discussed in this book. Vistage has over 16,000 CEO members in 15 countries and over 750 chair-coaches. More can be learned about Vistage by visiting its website at www.vistage.com.

There is no clear pathway or program to becoming an executive coach. Closing knowledge gaps and overcoming challenges are key for the aspiring coach progressing along one of the many paths available to gain coaching skills, knowledge, and experience. Many of these paths will still lack in-depth or comprehensive development of the skills needed to become an effective executive coach. Until there are programs designed to fully develop coaching skills, the profession is likely to remain fragmented, producing people who call themselves executive coaches but who lack the complete knowledge and skills required to be effective.

The next chapter will discuss what executive coaches need to know about business to be able to help top-level executives succeed.

Chapter 7: Competencies and Business Knowledge Of a Coach[4]

"Experience is a hard teacher because she gives the test first, the lesson afterwards."

Vernon Law

The explosive growth of executive coaching has opened the door for practitioners from a variety of disciplines and backgrounds to call themselves executive coaches. These practitioners bring with them a myriad of competencies and credentials that purportedly qualify them to coach executives. This has created a dilemma for executives seeking a coach to differentiate the qualified practitioners from those who are not.

There has yet to be developed a standardized model for executive coaching or a specific set of recognized credentials acceptable for an executive coach. Much academic research and many articles have addressed various competencies essential to an effective coach and the necessity of chemistry between a coach and coachee. This chapter will address the core competencies of a coach and, specifically, the need for an executive coach to have business

---

[4] This chapter is adapted from Weinstein, Alan G., and Jessica J. Schimert, 2007, *Business and Interpersonal Competencies of an Executive Coach*, CLADEA Proceedings.

119

knowledge and expertise in order to make his or her coaching successful.

Why Does an Executive Coach Need to Understand Business?

Executive coaching is an interactive, experiential process of inquiry characterized by personal discovery; it is a personal leadership-development process. Coaching is considered a process because it facilitates an ongoing evolution of an individual from a current state toward a desired state. The process includes equipping coachees with tools, knowledge, and opportunities to develop themselves and to become more effective. This process must be directed toward a specific desired state or outcome. The desired state must be properly aligned with the strategy and goals of the coachee's organization.

Executive coaching implies that a coach must have a certain level of business knowledge and experience. The nature and depth of knowledge and experience will be specific to each coaching situation. For example, a CEO coachee may have different needs from a coach than a COO, an HR manager, or an IT manager. With that said, a case can be made that a coach must have broad, general business knowledge, skills, and experience rather than a specialized background.

It is important that an executive coach understand business for three reasons: to establish credibility, to communicate effectively, and to apply the coaching model. First and foremost, the coach/coachee relationship must be considered a partnership—based on mutual trust, mutual respect, and mutual freedom of expression—in which both parties are committed to achievement of the desired state or outcome. A coach with practical business knowledge and experience will be better able to gain the trust and respect of the coachee because the coach has been able to establish credibility. Being perceived as fully understanding the business challenges of the coachee will enable the coach to dig deeper into the relationship and offer more real-life examples, thus enhancing the coaching relationship.

Remember, the primary goal of the executive coaching process is to help the coachee achieve a desired outcome. In order to accomplish the goal, the coach and coachee must be able to speak a common language and understand the organizational context in which the current state is occurring.

The majority of the issues the coachee brings to the table are business related; therefore, it is important that both parties speak the same language: the language of business. Most executives want practical, results-oriented, efficient, and customized coaching. They are comfortable with a coach who speaks their language rather than one who is primarily theoretical, abstract, and didactic. Specifically, a coach who is experienced in business and able to articulate that knowledge in a concrete manner will be able to communicate with the executive on his or her terms via a common language. As I have repeated often, coaching involves reducing gaps between actual and desired behavior or performance. The coach's responsibility is to create tension around the gap in order for the coachee to work toward closing it. It is important for the coach to understand the coachee's assets and liabilities in order to help the executive become aware of his own balance sheet and strategically apply and develop his or her assets while managing liabilities. The coachee's balance sheet is an important aspect of the coaching process and fertile ground for the coachee to work. To the degree that gaps exist around business issues, the coach will need to understand these business issues and help the coachee identify ways to reduce the gap.

The ability to utilize the coaching model in order to help the client move from a current state to a desired state requires business acumen. The coach must be able to ask the right questions, encourage reflective insights and learning, and reframe the situation in order to create the tension necessary for change—and he or she must be able to quickly synthesize and process information and make good judgments and decisions. A lack of business knowledge and expertise would greatly hinder the ability to employ the coaching model and carry out productive conversations.

For example, the focal point of the coaching process is the gap between the coachee's desired behavior and his or her current behavior. The goal is to address the gap and modify the behavior. The gap creates tension that, in turn, becomes the motivation, or driver, toward action. One opportunity the coach has to add value is through proper diagnosis of the gap. The coach's responsibility is to provide a more objective, removed perspective; reframe the problem; and identify the root cause by asking effective questions and encouraging reflective learning. In other words, the gap may be a result of knowledge or skills deficiencies, the environment, personal attitudes and beliefs, or some combination of one or more of these factors. A competent coach will be able to correctly diagnose the source of the gap. A coach who lacks adequate business knowledge and experience will simply not have the tools to identify the gap and help reframe the situation for the coachee.

The coach must also be able to analyze assessments and present the results in a manner that relates to the coachee's current business situation. If the goal is to tie the desired change to the goals of the organization, then the coach must be able to make that connection based on knowledge and past experience. The coach must understand the job responsibilities of the coachee and the unique context and business objectives of the coachee's organization. By understanding both aspects of the situation, the coach can match the factors revealed by the coachee's balance sheet to the job responsibilities and organizational needs. Perhaps this point was best made by Thomas Saporito: "If senior executives are going to view developmental coaching as effective, it had better be evident to them that the efforts are intimately tied to the realities of the business" (Saporito 1996).

What Does a Coach Need to Understand about Business?

The following table lists six business competencies that an executive must possess (Weinstein and Bianchi 2000). An executive's coach must also be well versed in these competencies in order to establish credibility with the coachee, effectively communicate with him or her, and successfully apply the coaching model. Examples of the six business competencies an effective coach must possess—leadership, strategy, operational excellence, financial management, growth and challenge, and communication—are provided in the following table. Each of these competencies is discussed in detail and a case study provided to illustrate it.

Table 7-1: Executive Competencies

Competency	Example
Leadership	Capacity for vision; team development; understanding of group dynamics; ability to delegate; ability to develop, mentor, and motivate individuals and teams
Strategy	Marketing intelligence (including sales); organizational restructuring; board relations; labor relations; organizational strengths; mental maps; develop values, vision, and mission
Operational Excellence	Organizational development; human resource management; managing work flow; technology; product manufacturing
Financial Management	Read and interpret financial statements; manage cash flow; recognize key indicators; utilize financial ratios; have working knowledge of basic accounting principles; understand and manage financial institutions and partners
Growth and Challenge	Openness to change; adult learning theory; organizational learning; ethics and social responsibility; work/life balance; stress management; stages of growth
Communication	Empathy and emotional intelligence; effective listening and effective questioning; conflict management; providing feedback; clear and simple language

Leadership

An executive coach must have strong leadership skills because his or her primary job is to develop leaders. Leadership includes the capacity for vision, team development, understanding of group

125

dynamics, and the ability to delegate. Leadership also encompasses the ability to develop, mentor, and motivate people.

Case Study: An Introvert Learns to Lead

Joe was the general manager of a large distribution division of a publicly held corporation. He was not the stereotypical leader— bold, assertive, decisive, and confident. Instead, Joe was an introvert, quiet and slow at making decisions. He also had many strengths: he knew distribution thoroughly, he was a good strategic thinker, and he was perceived by his subordinates as highly credible. Joe inherited a politically charged executive team when he arrived at his division. His predecessor regularly played executives against each other and made separate deals with each of them. When Joe arrived, he knew he needed to take action, but his leadership liabilities stood out. He was not sure which way to turn.

Much of Joe's coaching was focused on identifying and managing his assets and liabilities. Once his balance sheet was established, Joe decided to rebuild his team with people who first were competent in their area of responsibility and secondly complemented his liabilities with their own strengths.

For example, Joe's HR director was so aligned with the previous GM that no one else on the executive team found him credible. Furthermore, the HR director was not doing the job Joe wanted him to do. Because Joe had a hard time firing people, a performance feedback model was developed for this HR director that clearly identified deliverables and deadlines to meet. When his HR director had difficulty meeting these objectives, Joe asked what was keeping him from doing so. In the ensuing conversation, the HR director resigned, stating he felt incompetent to perform as expected. The resignation was turned into a retirement, which pleased Joe and his HR director. One by one, Joe built his own team, each time upgrading the skill level and the strength of his team. They had many conversations about each of their assets and liabilities, and they learned to respect each other for their contributions to the team.

As this case illustrates, Joe was able to leverage his assets by building a strong team that complemented his strengths and offset his liabilities. He was also able to overcome his reluctance to fire a team member by benchmarking deliverables and setting a timetable for completion. Not being able to meet these expectations, team members chose to resign rather than be fired. Joe learned to ask good questions that made clear what constituted success and failure for his team. He was able to lead his division and replace his dysfunctional team with highly competent executives.

The company has had tremendous success, much of it attributable to the skill Joe displayed in building his team. The team members *turned out to be his disciples, cascading organizational goals down to the workers on the floor. Joe learned that he could lead with a supportive team that complemented his leadership style.*

This case illustrates the use of the coaching model to identify gaps. Specifically, the coach was able to analyze Joe's assets and liabilities and help Joe identify the leadership gap in his current and desired performance. Joe was then able to replicate the coaching model with his inherited team to identify team gaps and, ultimately, develop an effective team with complementary skill-sets.

Strategy

Executives should be heavily focused on developing the strategy for their organization. In order for a coach to properly add value to the coaching relationship, he or she must understand various levels of strategy, such as marketing intelligence (including sales), organizational restructuring, board relations, and labor relations. A coach must also have the ability to identify and leverage personal and organizational strengths, create mental maps of a business and its environment, and be able to articulate the values, vision, and mission of the organization. Finally, a coach must be able to understand what it takes to sustain a competitive advantage. How to innovate and stay ahead of the competition are important conceptual skills for a coach. In other words, the coach needs to be competent in strategic thinking that parallels what he or she is trying to coach the coachee to attain. In order to coach effectively, the coach must be familiar with the language, history, and current conditions of the executive's industry and business environment.

With that said, it is important for a coach to understand both the high level, "strategic" side of business and the tactical, "management" side of business because any strategy is useless without the ability to execute it. While it is important for the coach to consider the coachee's organization from both a high level and the ground level, it is also the coach's responsibility to ensure that the executive remains focused on strategy while delegating specific activities to the appropriate parties who will be able to execute them. The case below illustrates how coaching can help a coachee to think strategically.

Case Study: Coached for Strategic Thinking

Peter is the consummate entrepreneurial executive. Trained as an accountant, he began his early career at a top national accounting firm in the health care industry. After a few years, he was recruited by a hospital, at which he established a reputation as a very capable executive. In his next position, he navigated a regional hospital through a highly political and turbulent environment. During this time, he earned an MBA. In all of his work experiences, Peter developed skills in networking, negotiating, and strategic thinking. He saw the big picture in health care, and he knew where market niches existed and how to

129

access them. His networking ability allowed him to identify persons who could help him enter into relationships to support niche opportunities. These were Peter's assets, but he also had liabilities.

One liability was his attention to detail. So, when he took a position in a private for-profit health care company, he hired his former number-two person as COO of this company. By managing this liability, Peter was then able to design and guide the growth of this very small company. He began to leverage his networked relationships to obtain potential customers. He also developed new products with existing HMOs that were looking for products to differentiate themselves from competitors. When he struggled to get traction with large customers who questioned his company's size and ability, he circumvented these criticisms by forming strategic alliances with companies that already had relationships with these customers. Peter had a gift: he was able to develop mental maps of his industry and its players that allowed him to plot a strategy for achievement. These mental maps enabled him to move forward and grow his company. Peter constantly scanned his environment and identified strategic partners as well as niche markets that were either underserved or poorly served. He partnered with companies that had established networks and added both the scalable efficiencies of his company and new products to the offerings of these partners. He grew his organization from a small regional company to a larger company with a larger territory. After two years of laying the foundation of his company, his sales doubled during the next two years.

The primary role of Peter's coach was to keep him focused on his strategic objectives. Understanding how Peter's mind worked, his coach continually probed about opportunities, questioned how they fit his strategy, and helped Peter become aware of how to leverage his strengths in the pursuit of strategic opportunities. This enabled his company to grow its markets and absorb this growth under the very capable executive in charge of operations. The coach's knowledge about strategy was critical in helping Peter grow his company.

Operational Excellence

With respect to operational excellence, an effective coach must understand organizational development, human resource management, technology, and product manufacturing. Organizational development primarily refers to the ability to manage change within an organization. Human resource management refers to the ability to recruit, hire, train, and retain the best employees. As Jim Collins aptly puts it in *Good to Great* (2001), it is important to "get the right people on the bus." Effective HR management is not simply a matter of utilizing effective financial compensation. In order to hire the best and keep them happy, a company must identify alternative motivators that can be used to satisfy employees' individual needs. For example, a career development plan, challenging and supportive work environment, and appropriate recognition may be implemented on an individual basis to help retain the best and the brightest.

A coach must also have some understanding of the technology of operations, including systems integration, software systems, and information technology. He or she must also be familiar with product development, manufacturing, research and development, and quality and process management. It is important for the coach to be aware of how product innovation fits into the overall operations of the organization. Finally, understanding methodologies of operational efficiency will help when dealing with the challenges of costs and on-time delivery of products. This knowledge is vital for the coach to be able to share with the coachee in the context of the coachee's organization and its competitors, and ensuring that the coachee is helping the company remain ahead of the curve.

Case Study: Operational Effectiveness through Coaching

Mark is an engineer who took over a garage-based business from his father and turned it into a growing manufacturing company with 200 employees and a state-of-the-art factory. Mark's major customers are manufacturers of vehicles. His success came mostly from patented products that his company designed and developed in-house. With intense competition from China looming, Mark was concerned about his costs and his ability to maintain business after his patents expire. At the same time, customers wanted Mark's company to constantly cut its costs, making it difficult to innovate and create the next generation of products. Innovation requires a special environment without the pressures of deadlines and production schedules. In fact, auto manufacturers demanded to see Mark's cost information so they could participate in cost-cutting efforts.

Realizing his future lay in new product development, Mark needed a structure to solve this paradox between the needs for innovation and low-cost manufacturing. Many sessions were spent with his coach exploring options about how to do this. Then Mark came up with a brilliant plan: he created a task force, which he called his "Pioneer Team." This group was charged with new product development. He put his most innovative people on this team. A second, smaller team was charged with taking the Pioneer Team designs and creating models and prototypes of its designs. They were also charged with testing these designs using rigorous quality and endurance standards. The remaining operations people were charged with continuing to concentrate on low-cost manufacturing. Their role was to create efficiencies, cut waste, and strip unnecessary costs from the operations and the product.

By separating these three functions, Mark's company was able to focus on three different processes and protect each from the incompatibilities of the others. He was able to produce low-cost products and innovate. In most organizations, these goals get blended into one, losing focus on the unique requirements of each and often failing to do either one of them well. In Mark's plant, his operations team was able to cut costs in manufacturing processes and materials without sacrificing quality. They also vertically integrated their operation through an acquisition that enabled them to control supplier costs. All this was accomplished through an organizational design that protected otherwise incompatible functions from interfering with each other. Mark's company continues to grow in the highly competitive marketplace of vehicle manufacturing.

The role of coaching in Mark's case was to help him redesign his organization to meet seemingly incompatible strategies. The coach's understanding of organizational design helped Mark to solve the problem that could have threatened his business.

Financial Management

Understanding corporate financial statements and how financial institutions work is an essential aspect of financial knowledge for a coach. A competent coach must be able to read and interpret financial statements, understand the principles of managing cash flow, recognize key indicators (such as receivables and inventory), utilize financial ratios, and have a working knowledge of basic accounting principles. The ability to develop and gauge a financial "dashboard" is also helpful in a coaching scenario. The dashboard may serve as a roadmap to keep all parties involved in a coaching relationship clearly informed and on track with the company's progress.

A coach should also be skilled at working with and managing accountants and financial institutions. Too often, business leaders put full trust in their accountants and bankers and never question their decisions. It is crucial that a business leader maintain control over financial partners to ensure his best interests are always considered. A coach who fully understands financial management will be able to evaluate how well the coachee is managing any financial responsibilities within his or her organization.

Case Study: Coaching for Financial Literacy

John was getting mixed advice from several advisors, including family members who were entrepreneurs and experienced executives, and his own accountant. Several years earlier, John made an acquisition to add a complementary product to his service line. With his accountant's blessing, he paid for this acquisition out of his revolving credit line. This loan made his bank nervous, and it decided to fire him as a customer.

The fundamental problem the bank saw was John's cash flow, which was strained due to the acquisition costs. The new interest accrued on the loan was becoming burdensome. Every year was getting a little better, but John's cash flow was still poor, and he was personally struggling with what he now considered a bad acquisition. With coaching, John began to understand the cause of the problem. John's coach, who was skilled in financing management, was able to allow John to see that his payment for the acquisition was based on optimistic sales results. John also saw that he did not have a contingency plan for lower sales, and he underestimated the cost of these sales. John's coach allowed him to see that he had gotten bad advice—not so much for making the acquisition but in the way he had financed it.

After understanding the causes of his problem and projecting out his cash flows over the next two years, John realized his problem was short term. John's coach helped him to realize that the acquisition was making money as well as being synergistic with his other services. John then found a bank willing to work with him, and he is now financially healthy. Through coaching, John learned how to better finance his acquisitions and make contingency plans in case the acquisition was slow in realizing its potential. Several years later, John was able to put these lessons to use in making a major acquisition.

The above case illustrates the need to understand finances and be able to manage cash flow. The coach was able to help John realize the importance of cash flow, understand the variety of financing options to maintain it, and develop a contingency plan for the slower-than-expected sales projections.

Growth and Challenge

In order for an executive coach to be successful, he or she must be competent in conveying the skills collectively known as "growth and challenge" to his or her coachee. Growth and challenge skills include openness to change, knowledge of how adults learn, organizational learning, ethics and social responsibility, work/life balance, stress management, and recognition of the stages of personal as well as organizational growth. The executive coaching process is always an evolution, and both parties must be prepared to deal with the continual change brought about by coaching in order for growth to occur.

The following case illustrates one element of growth, the stages of development, and how it affects critical relationships with a vendor and customer.

Case Study: Growing through the Stages of Development

Steve had grown his sales at about 5 percent per year for several years. In the past two years, this rate of growth had increased to 15 to 20 percent. There were good reasons for this growth: the industry was growing and his company had successfully entered a new market where demand was strong for its products. This growth led to a new factory facility, new machinery, and the growth of the executive staff. Steve had just received a major order, the largest in company history. He approached his bank for an increase in his company's line of credit to be able to manufacture and ship this order.

The bank said no.

Steve's company had been a customer of the bank for many years, and he had always had a great relationship with it. But the bank wanted Steve to put in more equity, even though the company was not heavily leveraged with debt. Through coaching, it became apparent that Steve was dealing with one of the areas of growth that scares banks—debt to equity ratios. Growth requires capital, and banks, while supplying debt financing, do not like to exceed their limits. Steve was also dealing with the small business loan department of the bank, and he was nearing his limit on borrowing for this division.

His coach was aware that this could be a problem. In the dialogue between Steve and his coach, Steve put his anger and disappointment aside and started to understand what was really driving the bank's decision-making process. The bank's loan department wanted to keep Steve as a customer because he paid a lot of interest and fees. But they were near their limit on how much they could lend him. Needing better financing to grow his company led Steve to shop his credit needs with other banks. He learned through coaching that his loyalty was misplaced in a situation for which the rules had changed. His expectation that his bank would stand by him as he grew his company had changed to a more realistic view of how banks operate. To Steve, growth was a great opportunity. To his bank, it was cause for concern.

His coach assisted Steve by helping him to understand his company's growth process with respect to bank financing. The coach's knowledge about banking and growth needs helped to guide Steve toward an approach to solve his problem and fuel his company's growth.

Communication

The technical competencies, or "nuts and bolts," of business have been discussed in some detail thus far. However, in order for a coach to be successful, he or she must also embody emotional intelligence and effective communication skills. A coach must be a competent communicator at all levels: interpersonally, within a group, and organizationally. Specific communication skills that are necessary for any coach include active listening, effective questioning (or the ability to probe), the use of clear and simple language, reframing, and giving and receiving feedback. In communicating, a coach must be willing to challenge and able to maintain focus. It is also necessary for a coach to understand, and oftentimes be able to employ, conflict mediation skills, persuasion tactics, and negotiation strategies.

Communication skills are necessary to employ the coaching model. It is the coach's responsibility to engage the coachee through questioning. By asking effective questions, the coach can begin to identify the performance gap. Continued probing and active listening will help to establish the tension created by the gap. Once the tension is identified, the coach must guide the coachee toward the solution with strategic communication. It is important for the coach to keep the coachee focused on problem-solving during the probing and confrontation rather than defending himself or herself. The coach must remember that he or she is a facilitator and must keep the coachee working toward resolving his or her gap and not simply reacting to it.

Emotional intelligence is an essential competency of any executive coach, especially as he or she communicates with the coachee. The coaching model requires a coach to probe deeply and confront the coachee; however, the coach must have a keen awareness of his or her role, the coachee, and the situation in order to determine when and how deeply to probe. Confrontation must be conducted in a caring manner in order to achieve desired results.

An important skill for coaches is the ability to format questions that lead to favorable results. Effective questions often begin with the words or phrases *what, how,* and *tell me more about.* These questions move the dialogue toward clarity and problem-solving. Effective questions concentrate on eliciting answers around what's already working, clarifying objectives, and agreeing on next steps. Effective questions are energizing and supportive; they create a clear target or goal and turn coercion into collaboration. Effective questions move people forward and provide them with the sense of how they can create their own results; the coach who uses effective questions is facilitating a constructive conversation.

How a coach phrases questions can also have a negative impact. Some questions, such as those beginning with the word *why,* can elicit excuses that keep a coachee from accepting full responsibility for actions or events. Questions beginning with *when* can lead to the coachee delaying action or putting things off if not related to specific goals. And questions beginning with *who* have a tendency to lead to scapegoating and should be avoided. As shown in the following case, effective questions are a key component of the communication strategy of any successful coaching relationship.

Case Study: Listening as a Crucial Step toward Communication

Bill was CEO of a mid-sized insurance company. He held staff meetings every Wednesday morning at 8:30 a.m. sharp. The stated purpose of these meetings was to review strategic initiatives and communicate how each executive was performing on his or her goals. Unfortunately, what was really happening at these meetings was a freestyle critique of team members, who blamed each other for failing to reach stated goals. The meetings were tense and frustrating for Bill.

After the meetings ended, executives were known to continue talking about each other and critiquing what was said or not said at the meeting. Low morale was permeating the organization. Following an organizational survey that revealed a high level of dissatisfaction among his associates, Bill decided to confront this issue head on. He brought in a coach/facilitator to open up communication and develop ground rules for more effective meetings. After several meetings in which the executives engaged in open conversation about their group process, they committed to a better process that embraced healthy conflict—discussion that was not personal but instead constructive and focused toward goal attainment. All participants also agreed not to complain about the meeting after it ended. With a few exceptions, the team embraced this new process and showed progress in meeting organizational goals.

Bill continued working with his coach to develop better communication with each executive on his team. He responded well to tailoring his communication methods based on the individual styles of each team member. Most of all, Bill engaged in *active listening, helping him develop a deeper understanding of his executives. The latest organizational survey of his associates showed a marked improvement in satisfaction and morale. The company revenues and bottom line also showed significant improvement.*

In this case, the coach acted as a team facilitator, helping to establish group norms and codes of conduct that were constructive toward the company's stated purpose. When the team facilitation was completed, the coach was retained to work with the CEO to maintain improved communication, allowing him to work on sustaining the team improvements. Many of the subsequent coaching sessions involved reflections of situations, allowing the CEO to continually monitor his communication and team leadership and coach his team members to be more effective both in groups and as role models for others.

Conclusions

Although executive coaching is an emerging field, a core of competencies has emerged as crucial to the success of any coaching relationship. An executive coach needs to have business knowledge and expertise in order to establish credibility with the coachee, effectively communicate with him or her, and successfully apply the coaching model. Furthermore, the depth of the six specific business competencies an executive coach possesses—leadership, strategy, operational excellence, financial management, growth and challenge, and communication—will determine his or her success in helping coachees achieve their maximum potential.

Chapter 8: Summary and Conclusions

"There are people who live their whole lives on the default setting, never realizing you can customize."
Robert Brault

Executive coaching is emerging as one of the most powerful approaches to executive development. In the previous chapters, I have tried to create a model of executive coaching that incorporates the changes, skills, and knowledge that a coach needs to incorporate into the practice of coaching. Whether you are a coach looking for guidance or an executive wanting to know what constitutes effective coaching, this book is designed to help.

There is little question that strong leadership is needed to operate a successful organization. Executive coaching can be a key to developing that leadership. Executive coaching can be a difference-maker in helping leaders reach their full potential in moving their organizations forward.

Executive coaching is not a fix-it approach to executive development. When done well, executive coaching is designed to give high-potential executives the opportunity to grow and improve their effectiveness. It is a proactive process tailored to the specific assets and liabilities of the executive.

145

The heart of this book is in Chapter 2, where the coaching model is presented. At a developmental level, coaching can be described as creating tension that will motivate a coachee toward change. Focusing on gaps in performance between desired outcomes and current results will set the stage for change. In the hands of a skilled coach, the tension created by this gap will help the coachee to identify strategies to reduce the tension in ways that favor goal achievement. The role of the coach is not to solve the problems identified by the gap or to advise the coachee on how to succeed. Instead, it is to ask probing questions that require the coachee to find the answers and strategies that will lead to success. Many of the coach's tools to do this are discussed in Chapters 5 and 6.

If you think of a master detective, like Peter Falk's portrayal of Detective Colombo in the television series *Colombo*, you will recall the detective always asks "just one more question." Of course, each question is designed to create tension and, ultimately, trick the criminal into incriminating himself or herself with the goal of solving the mystery. Colombo could easily transfer this skill to executive coaching. What he has going for him are data and intuition. By piecing the puzzle together and asking questions, he is able to transform hunches into problem-solving. Similarly, coaching is an intuitive process that uses clues to drive toward resolution and results. By asking questions and following up on clues, the coach will help the coachee to reveal information that will lead to breakthroughs and actions.

The structural approach to coaching can be seen through the lens of the main players, the coach and the coachee. The role of the coach is to facilitate dialogue that allows the coachee to gain insights about behavior and to take appropriate actions to improve results. Several attributes of effective coaches were discussed. Intuitiveness allows a coach to pursue those clues that can lead to change on the coachee's part, much like Colombo. In following up those clues, a coach can guide the conversation toward creating tension that motivates the coachee toward action. While confrontational, these questions are always asked in the context of support and concern for the coachee. Trust and rapport are important in laying the groundwork for friendly confrontation.

Another attribute of the coach is the ability to reframe, or see a situation through a different perspective. This is often done by identifying a strength that can help a coachee to approach a situation from a new and powerful framework. Knowing one's assets and liabilities is an important step in being able to reframe. Other attributes of an effective coach are emotional intelligence, or the ability to be self-aware and to manage emotional states. It also allows a coach to engage others in a positive way.

Coachees need to gain insight into what drives their behavior. Their personality, approach to leadership, skills, attitudes, and aptitudes all impact how the coachee responds to others. There are several methods to uncover coachee attributes, including

147

psychological assessments, reflective insights from coaching, reading, or self-reflection. Feedback using 360-degree assessments can be revealing of how others view the coachee's style and behaviors. The purpose of assessments is to uncover clues as to the underlying causes of behavior. Assessments by themselves are merely clues. They need to be tested with the coachee's experience in order to validate their explanatory value. Assessments offer a deeper analysis of personality and behavioral style. They often yield insights that stimulate reflection. They reinforce the uniqueness of each individual. By comparing assessment results with real and reflected behavior, the mystery of the coachee's behavior reveals itself. This can be very useful to a coachee who suddenly has a language to understand the basis of his or her behavior.

Assessments are very helpful in building a coachee's balance sheet of assets and liabilities. Many professionally developed assessment measures help to identify assets as well as liabilities. The Strength Finder, developed by Buckingham and Clifton (2001) and based on thousands of executive responses, is particularly useful. It measures 34 potential strengths, reporting the top five as signature strengths. Chapter 3 reviewed several other assessment measures that can serve to open the coach/coachee dialogue toward building the coachee's balance sheet.

Because of the personal nature of coaching, assessment results and revelations from coaching should be considered confidential. Any reporting to sponsors of what goes on in coaching should be in summary form and with complete transparency with the coachee. Candor and trust can only exist under strict confidentiality. The proof of the effectiveness of coaching should only be presented with documentation of the results of coaching, not the coaching itself.

Situational factors that affect coaching can make a real difference in how a coach or coachee approaches alternative ways of making progress. For example, with a large percentage of businesses being family owned and managed, the context of coaching must be viewed from a systemic point of view. Family systems are emotional, whereas most businesses work best under a rational model of behavior. A coachee in a family business faces many challenges that are unique and complex. These situations need to be taken into account when coaching.

Among the more important distinctions about coaching is how it is different from consulting. I have tried to make this clear in several ways. First, coaches are not in the business of giving advice. Consultants are. Coaches should not be doing the mental "heavy lifting." Consultants are paid to do the heavy lifting. Coaches ask more questions than they answer. Consultants are paid to provide answers. Coaching uses methodologies such as reflection, reframing, and guided discussion. Consultants write and present reports filled with data and analyses. Coaches are intuitive and iterative. Consultants are methodical and generally use more structured methodologies.

Some of the challenges for coaches are to help their coaching clients to adopt new behaviors that will increase effectiveness. Among these behaviors are giving up control in order to get greater involvement of subordinates, delegation in order to share the workload, and relinquishing of authority to those lower in the organization. Micromanaging is one of the most frequent criticisms of coachees. This behavior is often driven by fear and lack of confidence in others. These behaviors have the potential to keep coachees from realizing their full potential.

I have emphasized the importance of intuition. Novice coaches often over-prepare questions and, by doing so, may miss real opportunities to go deeper in search of real tensions that the coachee may be experiencing. By being "in the moment" and less scripted, the coach is in a good position to pursue clues as they present themselves. Of course, active listening and good body language are additional characteristics that enable a coach to realize greater impact with coachees.

There is no standard practice when it comes to learning to become an executive coach. Most educational institutions fail to teach these skills. Private professional groups do put on programs that provide basic coaching skills, but many of these programs fail to follow an effective coaching model, such as the change model presented in this book. Coaching support groups can help to strengthen coaching skills. What is needed is a comprehensive program that not only elaborates on how to be an effective coach but also promotes mentoring and encourages feedback from peers on how the coach is performing in that role.

The last chapter identifies areas in business that coaches need to understand if they are to be effective. Imagine an executive coach who does not understand leadership, strategy, or operations. What if he or she could not read and understand financial statements? The career of a top-level executive involves multifunctional activities. If a coach is to help an executive gain mastery of these activities, the coach needs to understand the multifunctional nature of the executive's work role. This is in addition to understanding the so-called "softer side" of executive behavior—communicating, engaging, and facilitating insightful conversations. Business acumen without a strong set of coaching skills is not sufficient for a coach to be effective. Behavioral understanding and interpersonal skills, while helpful, are not sufficient to coach executives whose work life revolves around solving business problems. Both are needed for an executive coach to be effective.

In conclusion, executive coaching is a very complex process, requiring an understanding of human behavior and business. To do it well, a coach needs a model that will create change. The major responsibility for this change lies with the coachee. The role of the coach is to create tension between current performance and desired performance. The degree to which this tension seeks resolution will influence how much change will take place. The need for change will help the coachee to find alternative behaviors that are more effective than those that led to lower performance or poorer decisions. The coach needs to create an environment conducive to change. This is best done by asking probing questions and helping the coachee to change through reflection, reframing, and leveraging assets while managing liabilities. Executive coaching, when done well, will always make a difference. The many cases described in the chapters of this book are testimony of how coaching achieved just that: made a difference in the coachee's career and life.

Chapter 9: References

Baker, Dan, and Cameron Stauth, 2003, *What Happy People Know*, Rodale Press, Emmaus, Pennsylvania.

Bolman, Lee G., and Terrence E. Deal, 2001, *Leading with Soul*, Jossey-Bass, San Francisco, California.

Branham, Leigh, 2005, *The 7 Hidden Reasons Employees Leave: How To Recognize The Subtle Signs and Act before It's Too Late*, AMACOM Publishers, New York, New York.

Buckingham, Marcus, and Donald O. Clifton, Ph.D., 2001, *Now, Discover your Strengths*, Free Press, New York, New York.

Buckingham, Marcus, and Curt Coffman, 1999, *First, Break All the Rules*, Simon & Schuster, New York, New York.

Byham, William C.; Smith, Audrey B.; and Matthew J. Paese, n.d., *Grow Your Own Leaders, Acceleration Pools: A New Method of Succession Management*, DDI Press.

Carlson, Sune, 1951, *Executive Behavior: A Study of the Work Load and the Working Methods of Managing Directors,* Stromberg Publishing Co., Pine Lake, Minnesota.

Collins, Jim, 2001, *Good to Great*, Harper Collins, New York, New York.

Eichinger, R. W., and M. M. Lombardo, 2003, "360-degree Assessment," Knowledge Summary Series, Human Resources Planning, Volume 26, pp. 34-44.

Festinger, Leon, 1957, *A Theory of Cognitive Dissonance*, Stanford University Press, Palo Alto, California.

Fritz, Robert, 1984, *Path of Least Resistance: Learning to Become the Creative Force in Your Own Life*, Random House, New York, New York.

Genett, Donna M., Ph.D., 2004, *If You Want It Done Right, You Don't Have to Do It Yourself: the Power of Effective Delegation*, Quill Driver Books, Fresno, California.

Goleman, Daniel, Boyatzis, Richard E., and Annie McKee, 2002, *Primal Leadership: Learning to Lead with Emotional Intelligence*, Harvard Business School Publishing, Boston, Massachusetts.

Kahneman, Daniel, 2011, *Thinking Fast and Slow*, Farrar, Straus and Giroux, New York, New York.

Kotter, John P., 1996, *Leading Change,* Harvard Business Review Press, Cambridge, Massachusetts.

Mintzberg, Henry, 1973, *The Nature of Managerial Work*, Harper & Row, New York, New York.

Morgan, Howard; Phil Harkins, and Marshall Goldsmith, editors, 2004, *The Art and Practice of Leadership Coaching: 50 Top Executive Coaches Reveal Their Secrets*, John Wiley & Sons, New York, New York.

_____, 2003, *Profiles in Coaching: The 2004 Handbook of Best Practices in Leadership Coaching*, Linkage Press.

Neubauer, Peter B., and Alexander Neubauer, 1990, *Nature's Thumbprint: The New Genetics of Personality,* a Morningside Edition, Columbia University Press, New York, New York.

Pearl, Amy, Sharon Randaccio, and Alan G. Weinstein, 2010, *Using Assessment Tools to Enhance the Coaching Process*, an unpublished manuscript.

Quinn, Robert E., 2004, *Building the Bridge as You Walk on It,* Jossey-Bass, New York, New York.

_____, 1996, *Deep Change,* Jossey-Bass, New York, New York.

Right Management, Inc., 2011, *Why Global Leaders Succeed and Fail*, Right Management, Inc., Philadelphia, Pennsylvania.

Saporito, Thomas, 1996, "Business-Linked Executive Development," *Consulting Psychology Journal: Practice and Research*, Volume 56, Number 2 pp. 94-106.

Scott, Susan, 2002, *Fierce Conversations: Achieving Success at Work and in Life, One Conversation at a Time,* the Penguin Group, New York, New York.

Seligman, Martin E. P., Ph.D., 2006, *Learned Optimism*, Simon & Schuster, New York, New York.

_____, 2002, *Authentic Happiness*, Free Press, New York, New York.

Simon, Herbert, 1973, "The Structure of Ill Structured Problems," *Artificial Intelligence*, Elsevier, San Diego, California, Volume 4, Issues 3-4, pp. 181-201.

Weinstein, Alan G., and Jessica J. Schimert, 2007, *Business and Interpersonal Competencies of an Executive Coach*, CLADEA Proceedings.

Weinstein, Alan G., and Rita D. Markle, 2006, *A New Look at Executive Coaching: Reframing the Model*, an unpublished manuscript.

Weinstein, Alan G., and Carmen Bianchi, 2000, "Qualifications of the CEO in a Family Business," USASBE Proceedings, February 2000.

Made in the USA
San Bernardino, CA
12 July 2017